Binary Options

Fixed odds financial bets

by Hamish Raw

HARRIMAN HOUSE LTD

3A Penns Road
Petersfield
Hampshire
GU32 2EW
GREAT BRITAIN

Tel: +44 (0)1730 233870
Fax: +44 (0)1730 233880
Email: enquiries@harriman-house.com
Website: www.harriman-house.com

First published in Great Britain in 2008

978-1-905641-53-6

British Library Cataloguing in Publication Data
A CIP catalogue record for this book can be obtained from the British Library.

Printed and bound in Great Britain by Athenaeum Press Limited, Tyne & Wear.

Acknowledgements

To Professor Desmond Fitzgerald for introducing an itinerant truck driver to options theory. To Mark Levy and Danny Smyth, two of the slowest option pit traders I have ever had the pleasure of trading against, for reading through the manuscript and checking for glaring errors. To Stephen Eckett of Harriman House for direction. And finally to Cameron, Roxanna and Gabriella for persistently badgering their dad to finish the book.

Contents

Introduction 1

Section I 9
Chapter 1   Upbets & Downbets 11
Chapter 2   Theta & Time Decay 27
Chapter 3   Vega & Volatility 43
Chapter 4   Delta & Underlying 63
Chapter 5   Gamma & Delta 77

Section II 89
Chapter 6   Rangebets 91
Chapter 7   EachWayBets 109
Chapter 8   Eachway Rangebets 129

Section III 143
Chapter 9   Trading Binaries 145
Chapter 10 Hedging Binaries 165

Section IV 187
Chapter 11 One-Touch UpBets & DownBets 189
Chapter 12 No-Touch RangeBets 215
Chapter 13 Trading & Hedging 'One-Touch' Bets 231

Bibliography 243
Index 345

Introduction

Overview

As betting markets become more and more sophisticated (epitomised by the advent of specialist sports hedge funds) the crossover between sports betting and financial trading will intensify. Already futures trading by way of spreadbetting has become established in the sports betting market, while in turn fixed odds bets, by way of binary options, are being increasingly used for speculating in the financial and commodity markets.

Binary options (aka *financial fixed odds bets, aka binary bets*) have a number of characteristics which will enable them to become the most heavily used and popular derivatives instrument. They provide:

1. easy access for the trader via the internet;

2. a limited risk environment for all participants;

3. at expiry greater gearing for the speculator than, for instance, futures, CFDs, spreadbets or conventional options;

4. a far greater degree of flexibility enabling the sophisticated trader to customise his bet to take full advantage of accurate forecasts;

5. a product range that ranges from financial and commodity instruments to sports, political, media and weather; and finally

6. they are tax-free in many jurisdictions.

Binary options are used by people in many countries, albeit under a different name – that of a fixed odds bet. Nowadays many nations have their Kentucky Derby, Breeder's Cup, Grand National and Melbourne Cup, which attract wagers from a broad range of people; and recently betting on 'reality TV' events has become popular. All these betting participants are (unwittingly) buying binary options, and the flexible nature of this instrument will enable it to pervade the lives of many of whom are already avid sports punters but have always shied away from participating in the world of sophisticated financial instruments. Henceforth the term *fixed odds bet* will be interchangeable with the term *binary option* throughout this book.

Distribution

Hitherto, if one ignores fixed odds sports betting, binary options have been very much the preserve of the financial OTC (over-the-counter) market. Financial and commodity derivatives markets generally restrict themselves to offering futures and conventional options while the stock markets offer shares only. One must suspect the omission of binaries from derivatives markets has been an oversight, while from stock exchanges one suspects an attitude bordering on snobbery owing to the speculative nature of the instrument. Whatever the reason, these exchanges are likely to watch in awe as the trading volumes on binary/betting exchanges soar.

What are the grounds for such an assertion?

The following points explain why this instrument will see the same exponential growth that futures/options exchanges did throughout the latter half of the 1980s and most of the 1990s. The basic tenet springs from the fact that since binary option positions create a quantifiable maximum downside risk, this results in:

1 Risk Management

Conventional options are the most heavily exchange-traded option, yet volumes rarely exceed that of the underlying future with one or two exceptions (e.g. the Kospi index). This can be partly explained by the end-users' reticence in using a complicated instrument, but the major constraint is the reluctance of brokers to offer accounts to many customers who may not be capable of sustaining the potential losses that can be incurred from losing positions. These losing scenarios will always be predicated on the naked writing of options that occasionally explode, leaving the short with a potentially limitless, unrecoverable debit on his account.

In contrast to the above high-risk situation, the binary option enables all potential losses to be calculated on the inception of the trade, since the price of a binary option is constrained by the limits of 0 and 1. As we will see later, writing (selling) a binary call has the identical profit & loss (P&L) profile of buying the same strike put of the same series. On selling an out-of-the-money call at 0.2 (equivalent to a 4/1 bet) the seller's maximum loss will be at 1.0, where he will lose four times the amount he sold.

Clearly the broker is likely to have less unease in opening accounts for clients with this scenario; and if the broker insists on 100% upfront payment of the maximum potential loss, then the broker's potential liability is now totally covered.

2 Clearing and Settlement

A major constraint on starting and operating a derivatives exchange is the necessary cost of engaging a clearing house. The Eurex and the Chicago exchanges operate their own clearing houses, which require huge sums of cash in order to operate their exchanges with financial integrity. Clearly binary options alleviate this cost since the risk management is a more exact methodology. This is likely to lead to a proliferation of binary/betting exchanges globally.

3 Regulation

Regulatory authorities are placed between a rock and a hard place over the regulation of binary options exchanges. The nature of the risk involved means that these exchanges will distribute binary options via the internet in much the same way as eBay offers everything but bets via the internet. If regulation in any one jurisdiction becomes overburdensome then the exchange will up sticks and go offshore.

It is clear that the ability to distribute the product cheaply over the internet will be a major advantage to the exchange and the binary option user/trader. The combination of a homogenous, limited-risk instrument with zero credit facility ensures zero account defaults.

Leverage

The nature of binaries changes sharply as expiry nears. Shares and futures have linear P&L profiles that lie at a 45° angle to the horizontal axis. Conventional traded options have profiles that approach an angle of 45°. A 45° angle means that if the share/future/option goes up by 1¢, then the owner makes 1¢. A binary approaching expiry has a P&L profile that can exceed 45° (indeed it will approach the vertical for an at-the-money option) meaning that a 1¢ rise in the underlying share could translate into a multiple (say 5¢) increase in value of the option. Clearly this feature is likely to attract the player who is looking for short-term gearing, for it is safe to state that a binary option can provide greater gearing than any other financial instrument in the marketplace.

Dexterity

At present financial fixed odds betting suffers from a paucity of available strategies compared with conventional options. Spreadbetting companies' binary offerings are usually restricted to the regular upbets, downbets and rangebets in regular or one-touch/no-touch mode; but this is very plain fare in comparison to what's available on the high table of the OTC market. Knock-Out bets, Knock-In bets, Onions and bets on two separate assets are all available and over time are likely to, with one handle or another, enter the trader's vocabulary. Of course the trading community will require educating in order that they may use these instruments proficiently, but this is standard in all new markets. Once the trading community has a clearer understanding of binaries, there will no doubt be increased pressure on mainstream exchanges to issue binaries on their current products – with the CBOT's introduction of a binary on the Fed Funds rate the process has already started.

Product Sets

When considering binary options, the usual product revolves around foreign exchange bets and, more recently, bets on economic data and the aforementioned Fed Funds rate. Earlier in this introduction sports bets were proffered as alternative forms of binary options, but the product set need not end there. Bets on political events are prevalent particularly at the time of elections. Furthermore, the media is increasingly becoming a sector where wagers may be placed. Reality TV events are now widely accepted as a betting medium, but there is no reason why this should not be extended to, for instance, the film industry. Binary options on weekend cinema box office takings would no doubt be a welcome hedge for film producers and nervous actors.

Summary

Although this book steers clear of complex mathematics, it systematically analyses the anatomy of fixed odds bets. Hopefully this book will:

- allow the part-time punter to learn enough to eradicate amateurish mistakes;
- open up the financial and commodity fixed odds market to the sports betting enthusiast; and
- provide enough material and new concepts for the professional binary options trader to, at the very least, look at combining different forms of financial instruments with binaries in order to maximise potential profits and minimise unnecessary losses.

Section I:

This section introduces the reader to the two basic bets, the upbet and the downbet. These two bets are arguably the foundation for all financial engineering since any instrument can be broken down into a multiple of upbets or downbets.

In Chapter 1 the reader is initially introduced to the concept of when bets are winners and losers using random walk illustrations and P&L graphs.

Chapters 2 through to Chapter 4 inclusive are concerned with how upbet and downbet prices change owing to changes in the price of the underlying, changes in the volatility of the price of the underlying, plus time decay. These sensitivity analyses are known as the 'greeks' in options parlance.

1

Upbets & Downbets

1.0   Introduction

An upbet can only win or lose at the moment the bet expires and not at any time leading up to the expiry of the bet.

Examples of upbets are:

1. Will the price of the CBOT US Sep 10 year Notes future be above $114 at 1600hrs on the last trading day of August?

2. Will the Dow Jones Index be above 12,000 at 1600hrs on the last trading day of the year?

3. Will the LIFFE Euribor Dec/Sep spread be above 10 ticks at settlement on the last day of November?

4. Will a non-farm payroll number be above +150,000?

Examples 1, 2 & 3 enable the bettor to make a minute by minute assessment of the probability of the bet winning. Example 4 is a number (supposedly) cloaked in secrecy until the number is announced at 13.30 hrs on a Friday.

In all the above examples the bet always has a chance of winning or losing right up to the expiry of the bet although the probability may be less than 1% or greater than 99%. The Notes could be trading two full points below the strike the day before expiry but it is possible, although highly improbable, for them to rise enough during the final day to settle above the strike. Conversely the Notes could be trading a full two points higher than the strike the day prior to expiry and still lose although the probability of losing may be considered negligible.

Ultimately the upbet is not concluded until the bet has officially expired and until then no winners or losers can be determined.

Downbets too can only win or lose at expiry. Although in many circumstances the downbet is simply the reverse of the upbet, the downbet has been treated with the same methodology as the upbet in order that other bets, e.g. the eachwaybet, can be analysed within a uniform structure. Also a separate treatment of downbets will provide a firmer base on which to analyse the sensitivity of downbets.

1.1 Upbet Specification

Fig 1.1.1 presents three different random walks that have been generated in order to illustrate winning and losing bets. All the upbets start with an underlying price of $100, have twenty-five days to expiry and a strike price of $101.

1. Random Walk 1 (RW1) flirts with the $101 level after five days, retreats back to the $100 level, rises and passes through the $101 strike after eighteen days and then drifts to settle at a price around $100. The buyer of the upbet loses.

2. RW2 travels up to the $101 level after the eighth day where it moves sideways until, with nine days to expiry, the underlying resumes its upwards momentum. The underlying continues to rise and is around the $102.75 level at expiry, well above the strike of $101, so is consequently a winning bet with the seller ending the loser.

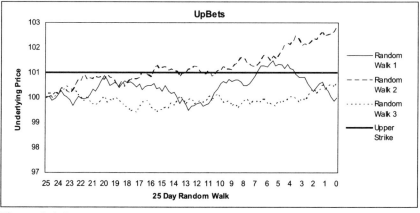

Figure 1.1.1

Upbets	Lose (0)	'Dead Heat' (50)	Win (100)
Random Walk 1	✓		
Random Walk 2			✓
Random Walk 3	✓		

3. RW3 drifts sideways from day one and never looks like reaching the strike. RW3 is a losing bet for the backer with the underlying settling around $100.50 at expiry.

1.2 Upbet Pricing

Fig 1.2.1 illustrates the expiry price profile of an upbet. One of the features of binaries is that at expiry, bets have a discontinuous distribution, i.e. there is a gap between the winning and losing bet price. Bets don't 'almost' win and settle at, say 99, but are 'black and white'; they've either (except in the case of a 'dead heat') won or lost and settle at either 100 or zero respectively.

1. If the upbet is in-the-money, i.e. in the above example of Fig 1.1.1 the underlying is higher than $101, then the upbet has won and has a value of 100.

2. Alternatively if the upbet is out-of-the-money, i.e. the underlying is lower than $101, then the upbet has lost and therefore has a value of zero.

3. In the case of the underlying finishing exactly on the strike price of $101, i.e. the upbet is at-the-money, then the bet may settle at 0, 50 or 100 depending on the rules or contract specification.

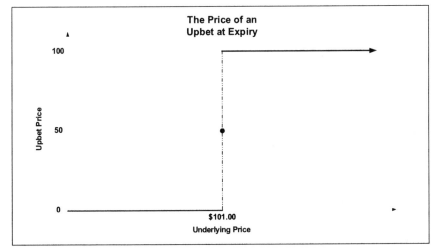

Figure 1.2.1

One issuer of binaries may stipulate that there are only two alternatives, a winning bet whereby the underlying has to finish above $101, or a losing bet whereby the underlying finishes below or exactly on $101. A second company might issue exactly the same binary but with the contract specification that if the underlying finishes exactly on the strike then the bet wins. A third company may consider that the underlying finishing exactly on the strike is a special case and call it a 'draw', 'tie' or 'dead heat', whereby the upbet will settle at 50. This company's rules therefore allow three possible upbet settlement prices at the expiry of the bet.

N.B. Throughout the examples in this book the latter approach will be adopted whereby in the event that a bet is a 'dead heat', or in other words, where the underlying is exactly on the strike price at expiry, then it is settled at 50.

1.3   Upbet Profit & Loss Profiles

The purchaser of a binary option, just like a conventional option, can only lose the amount spent on the premium. If Trader A paid 40 for an upbet at $1 per point then Trader A can lose a maximum of just 40 × $1 = $40. But with a binary not only the loss has a maximum limit but the potential profit has a maximum limit also. So although Trader A's loss is limited to $40, his profit is limited to (100 – 40) × $1 = $60. As a general rule the profit and loss of the buyer and seller of any binary must sum to 100 × $ per point.

In Figs 1.3.1 and 1.3.2 respectively Trader A's and Trader B's P&L profiles are illustrated. Both traders are taking opposite views on whether a share price will be above $101 at the expiry of the upbet.

In Fig 1.3.1 Trader A has bought the upbet at a price of 40 for $1 per point ($1/pt) so his three possible outcomes are:

1. Trader A loses $40 at any level of the underlying below $101.

2. At $101 the rules of this particular upbet determine a 'dead heat' has taken place and the upbet settles at 50 with Trader A making a profit of $10.

3. Above $101 Trader A wins outright and the upbet is settled at 100 to generate a profit of $60.

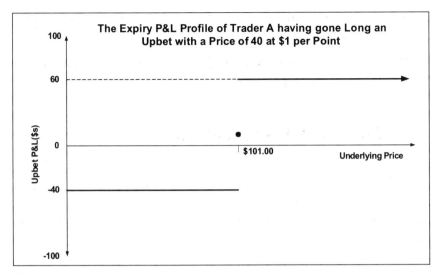

Figure 1.3.1

Trader B has sold this upbet at 40 for $1/pt so conversely Trader B's P&L profile is, as one would expect, the mirror image of Trader A's reflected through the horizontal axis.

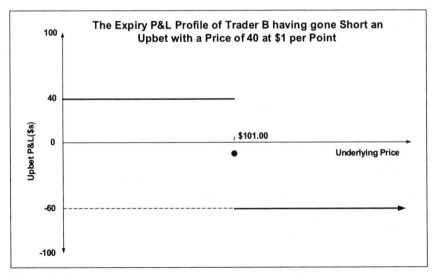

Figure 1.3.2

Trader B's three possible outcomes are:

1. Trader B has sold 40s and therefore wants to see the underlying below $101 where the upbet is worth zero at expiry and Trader B collects the premium of 40 × $1 = $40.

17

2. If the upbet settles at-the-money the upbet is worth 50 and Trader B loses $10 having gone 'short' $1/pt at 40.

3. The underlying is above $101 at the upbet's expiry so Trader B loses outright to the tune of $60.

1.4 Downbet Specification

The random walk model in Fig 1.4.1 describes when downbets win and lose. The starting point is yet again $100 with twenty-five days to expiry, except here the strike is $1 below at $99. In this instance the downbet is 'out-of-the-money' when the underlying is above the strike of $99 and 'in-the-money' below the strike.

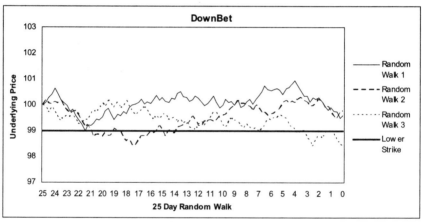

Figure 1.4.1

Upbets	Lose (0)	'Dead Heat' (50)	Win (100)
Random Walk 1	✓		
Random Walk 2	✓		
Random Walk 3			✓

1. After day three RW1 falls to $99.01 and bounces up. This is the closest RW1 gets to the strike and is trading at around $99.75 at the downbet expiry. Consequently RW1 closes out-of-the-money and is a losing bet.

2. RW2 initially falls to the $99 level in tandem with RW1 but breaches the strike. After ten days the underlying travels back up through the strike to trade alongside RW1 at expiry. Therefore this too is a losing bet.

3. RW3 trades down to the $99 level with seven days left. With three days to go RW3 trades back up to $99 from below the strike before making a final downward move on the last day to trade around $98.25 at expiry. This downbet closes in-the-money, and is a winning bet settling at 100.

1.5   Downbet Pricing

The expiry price profile of a downbet is illustrated in Fig 1.5.1. It is Fig 1.2.1 reflected through the vertical axis but with a strike of $99 as opposed to $101.

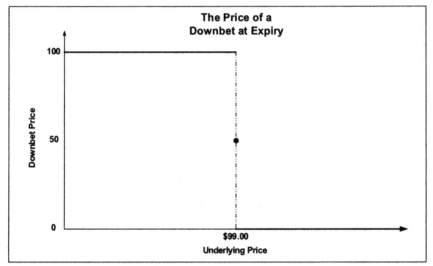

Figure 1.5.1

1. In this case if the underlying is above the strike of $99 at expiry, the downbet is out-of-the-money, has lost and is worth zero.

2. At $99 the downbet is at-the-money, is deemed a draw and worth 50.

3. While if the downbet expires with the underlying below the $99 strike, the downbet is in-the-money, has won and is worth 100.

1.6 Downbet Profit & Loss Profiles

Trader A and Trader B now decide to trade a downbet with each other. Trader A is no longer feeling bullish and wishes to buy a downbet (Fig 1.6.1) and since Trader B has conveniently turned bullish, he sells it to him. This is not an aggressive trade that Trader A is putting on; since the strike price is $101 and the underlying is $100 therefore the downbet is already $1 in-the-money and has a better than an 'evens money' chance of winning. The price of his downbet has to reflect this probability and the price is agreed at 60, where they trade for $1/pt.

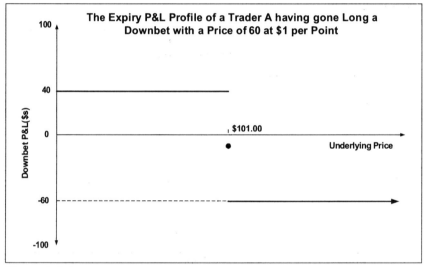

Figure 1.6.1

Trader A's maximum loss since he bought the downbet is 60 × $1 = $60, and this he will have to bear if the share price rises by over $1 from its current level of $100. His maximum potential winnings have been reduced to $40, which he will receive if the underlying either falls, stays where it is at $100, or rises less then $1. In other words Trader A has backed an 'odds-on' bet.

Fig 1.6.2 shows Trader B's profile having sold the in-the-money downbet to Trader A for 60. Trader B needs the share price to rise $1 in order to win. If the underlying rises exactly $1 to $101, then the downbet will be worth 50 and Trader B wins $10. A rise over $1 and the downbet expires with the underlying above $101 and Trader B collects the full $60.

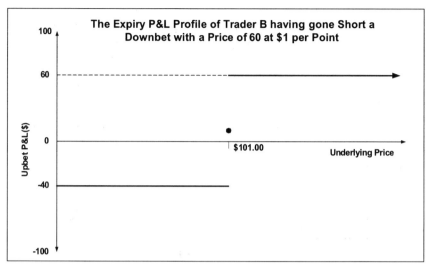

Figure 1.6.2

1.7 Up/Downbets v Conventional Calls/Puts

Some readers of this book will have an understanding of conventional options and may well find a comparison between binaries and conventionals of interest.

Upbets v Calls

In Fig 1.7.1 the price of the upbet and call are both 25 and both are worth $1 per point. Clearly the upbet's profit potential is limited to $75 with the 'draw' generating a profit of $25.

For the conventional call there is no limited upside, with the 45° profit line travelling upwards from –25 through breakeven, through 75, through 100 and upwards out of sight. But this increased potential profit comes at a cost, of course, because at any underlying price between A and B the conventional call performs less profitably than the upbet. At A, the upbet makes a 100% profit and turns a $25 bet into a $25 profit whereas the conventional option loses the full premium of $25.

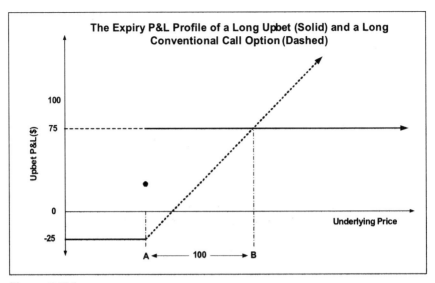

Figure 1.7.1

Where the conventional call breaks even at an underlying price 25¢ higher than A, the upbet is worth 100 generating a profit of 300%. The difference between the conventional and binary's profits subsequently diminishes until the underlying reaches B, where both conventional and upbet make a profit of $75. Above B the conventional call gains in value point for point with the underlying while the upbet is stuck on 100.

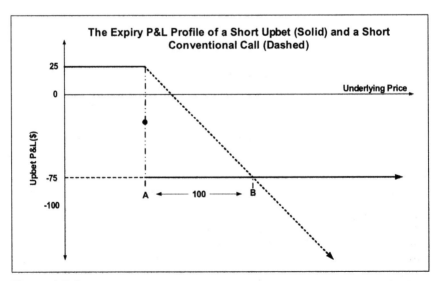

Figure 1.7.2

Fig 1.7.2 illustrates P&L profiles of the seller of the upbet and the writer of the conventional call. Here the profile of Fig 1.7.1 is reflected through the horizontal axis with the writer of the conventional losing less than the seller of the binary between A and B, but subsequently facing an unlimited loss scenario above B.

Downbets v Puts

Figs 1.7.3 and 1.7.4 illustrate the comparisons of long and short down-bet/put expiry P&Ls.

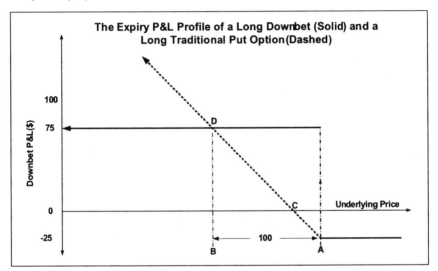

Figure 1.7.3

Assuming the price of the downbet and put options are both 25 and the strike at A is $99, then the trader who bought the conventional put has a breakeven at C where the underlying is equal to $99 – 25¢ = $98.75.

The breakeven for the downbet buyer is at A, the strike, where the downbet is worth 50 and the buyer doubles his money. At B, an underlying of $98, both conventional put and downbet make a profit of 300%, but lower than $98 the conventional is now behaving like a short future.

The scale of Fig 1.7.4 might suggest that a short conventional put has a limited downside. It does, at the point where the stock is worth zero. If the downbet and put options are worth $10/pt, then with the underlying at zero, the maximum loss for the downbet would be limited to:

$$\$10 \times (\,25 - 100\,) = -\,\$750;$$

whereas the maximum loss for the conventional put would be:

$$\$10 \times (0.00 - (\$99 - 25¢)) = -\$98,750.$$

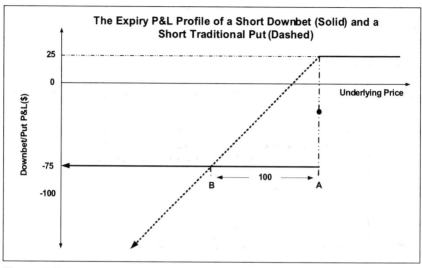

The Expiry P&L Profile of a Short Downbet (Solid) and a Short Traditional Put (Dashed)

Figure 1.7.4

The above comparisons between conventional calls, puts, upbets and downbets enable the user to further tailor the instrument to his market view. Furthermore, the combination of conventionals and binaries provides a highly sophisticated method of creating bespoke strategies for the imaginative and creative speculator.

1.8 Formulae

Upbet/Binary Call $= e^{-rt} N(d_2)$

Downbet/Binary Put $= e^{-rt} (1 - N(d_2))$

where $\qquad d_2 = \dfrac{\log(\frac{S}{E}) + (r - D - \frac{1}{2}\sigma^2)t}{\sigma\sqrt{t}}$

and

S = price of the underlying

E = strike/exercise price

r = risk free rate of interest

D = continuous dividend yield of underlying

t = time in years to expiry

σ = annualised standard deviation of asset returns

1.9   Summary

The probability of an event happening plus the probability of that same event not happening is 100%. Therefore, the probability that the share price at expiry ends up above $101, on $101, or below $101 must aggregate to 100%.

On comparing Fig 1.3.1 with Fig 1.6.2 and then Fig 1.3.2 with Fig 1.6.1 enables us to draw some interesting conclusions:

1. Selling an upbet for 40 is identical to buying a same strike, same expiry downbet for 60.

2. Buying an upbet for 40 is identical to selling a same strike, same expiry downbet for 60.

As a rule:

1. For the same strike and same expiry, BUYING an upbet for price X is the same as SELLING a downbet for 100 – X.

2. For the same strike and same expiry, SELLING an upbet for price Y is the same as BUYING a downbet for 100 – Y.

3. For the same strike and the same expiry the value of the upbet plus the value of the downbet must sum to 100. This rule may appear obvious and trivial but it absolutely differentiates binaries from conventional options as the section on vega demonstrates.

This chapter has covered the two most basic of binary instruments, the upbet and the downbet. The upbet and the downbet are the basic foundation blocks to which all financial instruments can be reduced.

1.10   Exercises

1. A bettor sells the out-of-the-money Comex Gold upbet at 28.2, $100 per point. What is the potential profit and loss?

2. The S&P Minis on the CME are trading at 1250. A punter fancies the market down. Should the aggressive gambler sell the 1350 upbet or buy the 1150 downbet?

3. The following prices are observed in the Forex $/€ binary options market for September expiry.

	Bid		Offer	
	Price	Size (per point)	Price	Size (per point)
120.00 Upbet	25.1	1000	27.6	3600
120.00 Downbet	65.1	5000	69.1	10000

If the underlying exchange rate is trading at $119.35, what trade(s) are available to lock in a profit? What will the profit be?

1.11 Answers

1. Potential profit = 28.2 × $100 = $2,820

   Potential loss = (28.2 – 100) × $100 = – $7,180

2. Buy the 1150 downbet since the emphasis is on the 'aggressive' gambler. Both bets are out-of-the-money and therefore worth less than 50. They both have strikes 100 from the underlying, so assuming a normal distribution, will be worth the same. Just say they were worth 25 each. Then selling the upbet can only ever realise a profit of 25 while buying the downbet at 25, will realise a profit of 75 should it win.

3. Firstly, the underlying in this case is irrelevant. Buying the upbet and the downbet will cost a total of 96.7 to yield a risk-free profit of 3.3, since the upbet and the downbet must aggregate to 100. Since this trade is risk-free 'fill yer boots' and do as many as possible, in this case $3,600 of each. Therefore:

   Profit = 3.3 × $3600 = $11,880

2

Theta &
Time Decay

2.0   Introduction

Theta is a ratio that measures how much the bet price will change due to the passing of time.

Theta is probably the easiest 'greek' to conceptually grasp and is possibly the most easily forecast since the passage of time itself moves in a reasonably uniform manner.

Bets on many financial instruments are now always 'in-running', i.e. there is always a market open on which to trade. These days there is a 24-hour market in foreign exchange trading so any bet on the future level of the $/£ rate is always 'in-running' with the theta constantly impacting on the price of bets. On other markets which operate in discrete time periods, where the market is open for a limited period of five days a week, market-makers will often use Monday's theoretical prices on a Friday afternoon in order not to get too exposed to the weekend's three-day time decay.

An understanding of time decay and theta is thus critical to the trading and risk management of binary options. The remainder of this section on theta will analyse the effect of time decay on upbets and downbets, and how this impact on the price of a bet is measured.

2.1   Upbets v the Underlying over Time

This section discusses time decay and its effect on the price of upbets as time to expiry decreases, ultimately resulting in the profile of Fig 1.2.1.

Fig 2.1.1 shows the profile of upbets with a strike price of $100 and a legend indicating the time to expiry. A unique characteristic of the binary is that, irrespective of whether upbet or downbet or time to expiry, each profile travels through the price 50 when the underlying is at-the-money, i.e. the underlying is exactly the price of the strike. This is because a symmetrical bell-shaped normal probability distribution is assumed so that when the underlying is at-the-money there is a 50:50 chance of the underlying going up or down. This feature of the binary immediately distinguishes it from the conventional option where the at-the-money can take any value.

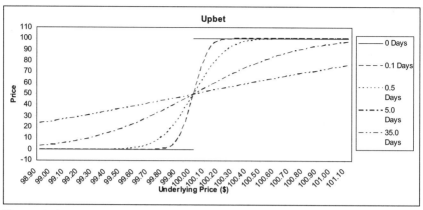

Figure 2.1.1

2.2 Price Decay and Theta

Fig 2.2.1 describes the prices of upbets with a strike price of $100 and time to expiry decreasing from 50 days to zero. In Fig 2.1.1 if one were to imagine a vertical line from the underlying of $99.70 intersecting 50 price profiles (instead of just the five listed in the legend) then in Fig 2.2.1 the middle graph would reflect those upbet prices against days to expiry.

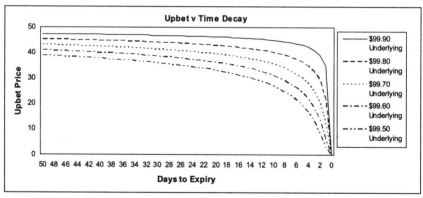

Figure 2.2.1

The $99.90 profile is always just 10 cents out-of-the-money and is always perceived to have good chance of being a winning bet. Only over the last day does time erosion really take effect with a near precipitous price fall from 35 to zero. The $99.50 profile paints a different picture as this upbet is always 50¢ out-of-the-money and the market gives up on the bet at an earlier stage. On comparing the gradients of the $99.90 and $99.50 profiles, the former has a shallower gradient than the $99.50 profile for most of the period but then as expiry approaches, this relationship reverses as the gradient of the $99.90 profile increases and becomes more steeply sloping than the $99.50 profile.

This gradient that we are referring to in Fig 2.2.1 is known as the theta. The theta of an option is defined by:

$$\theta = \delta P / \delta t$$

where: P = price of the option, and

t = time to expiry

so that δP = a change in the value of P

and δt = a change in the value of t.

The theta is therefore the ratio of the change in the price of the option brought on by a change in the time to expiry of the option.

To provide a more graphic illustration Fig 2.2.2 illustrates how the slopes of the time decay approach the value of the theta as the incremental amount of time either side of the 2 days to expiry is reduced to zero. The gradient can be calculated from the following formula:

$$\theta = (P_0 - P_1)/(T_1 - T_0) \times 365/100$$

where: P_0 = Price at time 0

P_1 = Price at time 1

T_0 = Time to expiry at time 0

T_1 = Time to expiry at time 1

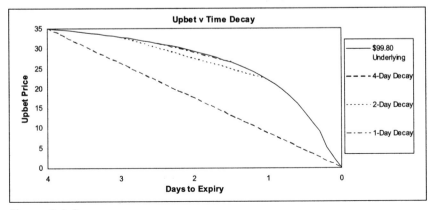

Figure 2.2.2

Table 2.2.1 shows the value of the bet as the days to expiry decreases from 4 to 0 with the underlying at $99.80. The theta with 2 days to expiry is actually –16.936 and this is the gradient of the tangent of the curve '$99.80 Underlying' in Fig 2.2.2 with exactly 2 days to expiry.

	Days to Expiry						
	4	3	2.5	2	1.5	1	0
				Gradient			
$\delta t = 0$				–16.936			
$\delta t = 0.5$			31.35	–17.484	26.56		
$\delta t = 1.0$		32.86		–19.491		22.18	
$\delta t = 2.0$	35.01			–31.947			0

Table 2.2.1

Thus, the 4-Day Decay line runs from 35.01 to zero in a straight line and has an annualised gradient of:

$$\text{Gradient of 4-Day Decay} = (0 - 35.01) / (4 - 0) \times 365 / 100$$
$$= -31.947$$

Likewise for the 2-Day & 1-Day Gradients:

$$\text{Gradient of 2-Day Decay} = (22.18 - 32.86) / (3 - 1) \times 365 / 100$$
$$= -19.491$$

$$\text{Gradient of 1-Day Decay} = (26.56 - 31.35) / (2.5 - 1.5) \times 365 / 100$$
$$= -17.484$$

The theta with $\delta t = 2$ days, 1 day and .5 day is –31.947, –19.491 and –17.484 respectively. As the time either side of 2 days to expiry decreases, i.e. as δt the theta approaches the value –16.936, the exact slope of the tangent to the curve at 2 days to expiry.

The next sections on upbet thetas describe how the trader can use this measure of time decay in a practical manner.

2.3   Upbet Theta

Table 2.3.1 provides 1 and 5 day thetas for underlying prices ranging from $99.50 to $99.90 and assumes a strike price of $100 and therefore applies to Fig 2.2.1. The theta for the $99.70 profile with 5 days left to expiry is –6.5057. This value of theta defines how much the upbet will decline in value over one year at the current rate of decay. To gauge how much the upbet will lose in time decay over 1-day divide the theta by 365 so the rough estimate of one-day decay at 5 days would be – 6.5057 / 365 = –0.017824. But remember, by convention binary prices are multiplied by 100 to establish trading prices within a range of 0 – 100, so likewise we need to multiply the theta by 100 to get comparable decay. In effect the time decay over 1 day of an upbet with 5 days to expiry is –0.017824 × 100 = –1.7824 points. In fact the upbet with 5.5 and 4.5 days to expiry is worth 28.2877 and 26.2938 respectively, a decay of –1.9939, so it can be argued that a 5-day theta of –1.7824 is a reasonably accurate measure.

	Underlying Price				
	$99.50	$99.60	$99.70	$99.80	$99.90
1 Day	–22.2051	–34.4148	–43.1305	–41.4541	–25.7706
5 Days	–8.5914	–7.8385	–6.5057	–4.6535	–2.4102

Table 2.3.1

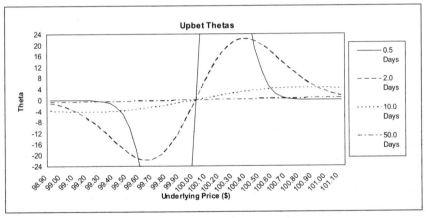

Figure 2.3.1

Fig 2.3.1 illustrates how thetas change with the underlying. The assumed strike price is $100 and four separate times to expiry are displayed.

1. It is apparent how little effect time has on the price of an upbet with 50 days to expiry as the 50-day profile is almost flat around the zero theta level.

2. Another point of note is that theta is always zero when the binary is at-the-money. In hindsight this should be reasonably obvious since it has already been pointed out that an at-the-money binary is always worth 50.

3. What may not be so apparent is that totally unlike a conventional option the theta of a binary may be positive as well as negative. This is because an in-the-money binary will have a price moving upwards to 100 as time decays and hence a positive theta, compared to the conventional that always has a negative theta.

As time passes and the upbet gets closer to expiry the absolute value of the theta becomes so high that it fails to realistically represent the time decay of the binary. From Table 2.3.1 the 1-day theta with the underlying at $99.70 is –43.1305 when the upbet value is actually 12.52. The theta is forecasting a decay of:

$$100 \times - 43.1305 / 365 = - 11.8166$$

which is not so far wide of the mark since it will in fact be –12.52 being the price of this out-of-the-money bet with 1 day to expiry. Should the 0.1 days to expiry profile be included, at an underlying price of $99.92 the theta would be –440.7 and the clarity of Fig 2.3.1 would be destroyed as the graph is drastically rescaled. It would also be suggesting that the upbet would lose:

$$100 \times - 440.7 / 365 = - 120.74 \text{ points}$$

over the day when the maximum value of an upbet can only be 100 and, with 0.1 days to expiry this bet would be in fact worth just 16.67.

In general the theta will always underestimate the decay from one day to the next since as can be seen from Fig 2.2.2 the slope of the profiles always gets steeper approaching expiry. This means that the theta, which could be construed as the average price decay at that point, will always over-estimate the time decay that has taken place over the preceding day but will under-estimate the decay that will occur over the following day. When there is less than one day to expiry the theta becomes totally unreliable.

Nevertheless, this mathematical weakness does not render the theta a totally discredited measure. Should a more accurate measure of theta be required when using theta to evaluate one-day price decay, a rough and ready solution would be to subtract half a day when inputting the number of days to expiry. If this offends the purist then another alternative would be to evaluate the bet at present plus with a day less to expiry. The difference when divided by 100 and multiplied by 365 will provide an accurate 1-day theta. This might at first sight appear to defeat the object of the exercise since one is calculating theta from absolute price decay when theta would generally be used to evaluate the decay itself, but it is an accurate and practical method for a marketmaker who is hedging bets with other bets.

The lack of accuracy of thetas close to expiry is not a problem exclusive to binary options but affects conventional options also. Even so conventional options traders still keep a 'weather-eye' on the theta, warts and all.

2.4   Downbets over Time

Fig 2.4.1 provides the route over time by which the downbet reaches the expiry profile of Fig 1.5.1. The time to expiry has been expanded in order to include a yearly binary. In this example if the underlying now falls from $100 to $98 the one year downbet only increases to 66.61. The best bit is that if you are long the one year downbet and the market rallies from $100 to $102 the downbet only falls to 35.53. Earlier during the book's introduction binaries were deemed to be highly dextrous instruments; this example proves that even the most dull, conservative, risk-averse pension fund manager who doesn't have the stomach for the standard +45° P&L profile of AAA-rated multinational stock can find, in the short term, a more boring, safer way to gain exposure to financial instruments.

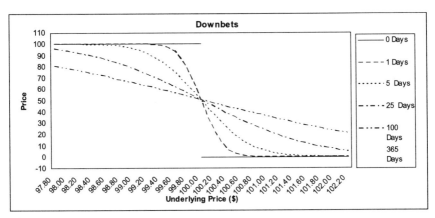

Figure 2.4.1

2.5 Downbet Theta

The downbet theta is the negative of the same strike upbet theta. Table 2.5.1 provides thetas for $100 strike downbets. They are all positive. This is because with the given range of underlying every downbet is in-the-money since the strike is $100 and the underlying is less than the strike. All in-the-money bets settle at 100 therefore each of the downbets in the table will increase in value as time passes.

	Underlying Price				
	$98.75	$99.00	$99.25	$99.50	$99.75
5 Days	3.0828	5.6843	8.1397	8.5914	5.6380
10 Days	3.4549	4.1940	4.3426	3.6365	2.0722

Table 2.5.1

With 10 days to expiry the highest theta in the table occurs when the underlying is $99.25 while, with 5 days to expiry, the highest theta occurs at $99.50. Clearly, unlike a conventional option where the highest theta remains static at the strike over time, with a binary the highest theta shifts towards the strike over time.

Fig 2.5.1 illustrates the downbet thetas where clearly the peak and trough of the theta approach the strike as time erodes. The theta of the 50-day binary is zero across the underlying range indicating that, irrespective of the underlying, the passage of time has zero impact on the price of the bet.

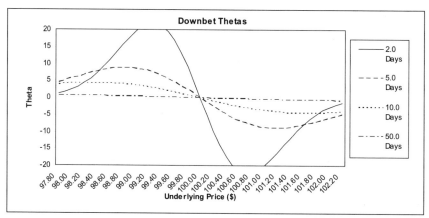

Figure 2.5.1

2.6 Theta and Extreme Time

Extreme time has been introduced as a special case since it should not divert attention away from the 'normal' characteristic of theta as outlined in Section 2.2. Nevertheless it would be remiss of a study of binary theta if the following quirk of theta was not acknowledged.

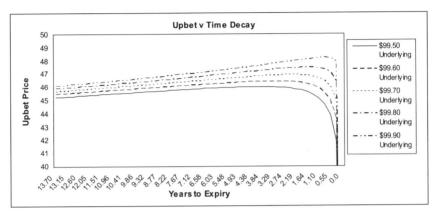

Figure 2.6.1

When there is a large amount of time to the expiry of the bet then theta behaves in an unusual manner. Fig 2.6.1 is Fig 2.2.1 but with a different time scale along the horizontal axis. The horizontal axis is now expressed in years and what the graph illustrates is that as time to expiry increases for an out-of-the-money upbet, the value of the upbet decreases. This implies that the curious situation would exist whereby an investor could buy the upbet with years to expiry, hope that the underlying does not rise, and still see his investment increase in value over time. In effect, the out-of-the-money upbet with sufficient time remaining to expiry has a positive theta.

The more ambitious reader may wish to shut their eyes and try and figure this one out, but for those of whom want to push on to the next subject here's the intuitive answer. This out-of-the-money upbet is constrained by the prices zero and 50. However close the underlying gets to the strike and irrespective of how much time is specified in the contract, the upbet cannot breach 50. And on the downside the probability of an event can never be negative so the upbet is restricted to zero. Increasing the time to expiry therefore has a decreasing effect on the price of the upbet close to the strike, as the probability of the upbet travelling through the strike cannot exceed 50%. But at the same time the increased time increases the probability of the underlying travelling to zero thereby ensuring a losing bet. Obviously this extreme case applies to downbets as well.

Is this quirk of any relevance? Probably not a lot. But consider an insurance contract (binary option) written at Lloyd's of London…a contract with a lengthy 'tail'. Food for thought?

2.7 Bets v Conventionals

Fig 2.7.1 provides a comparison of thetas for upbets, downbets and conventional calls and puts.

Points of note are:

1. Downbets and upbets mirror each other across the horizontal axis.

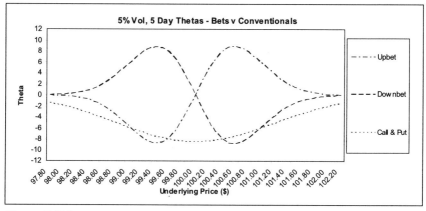

Figure 2.7.1

2. Whereas the theta of the conventional call and put are the same and are always negative, the theta of upbets and downbets each take on both positive and negative values.

3. The theta of the conventional is at its greatest absolute value where the theta of upbets and downbets are both zero, i.e. when the options are at-the-money.

38

2.8 Formulae

Upbet/Binary Call Theta $= re^{-rt} N(d_2) + e^{-rt}N'(d_2) \left(\frac{d_1}{2t} - \frac{r-D}{\sigma\sqrt{t}}\right)$

Downbet/Binary Put Theta $= re^{-rt} (1 - N(d_2)) - e^{-rt}N'(d_2) \left(\frac{d_1}{2t} - \frac{r-D}{\sigma\sqrt{t}}\right)$

where $= d_1 = \dfrac{\log(\frac{S}{E}) + (r - D + \frac{1}{2}\sigma^2)t}{\sigma\sqrt{t}}$

$$d_2 = \frac{\log(\frac{S}{E}) + (r - D - \frac{1}{2}\sigma^2)t}{\sigma\sqrt{t}}$$

$$N'(x) = \frac{1}{\sqrt{2\pi}} e^{-0.5x^2}$$

and

S = price of the underlying

E = strike/exercise price

r = risk free rate of interest

D = continuous dividend yield of underlying

t = time in years to expiry

σ = annualised standard deviation of asset returns

2.9 Summary

The theta is an immensely important 'greek' since it is always impacting on the value of a bet even should the underlying market be closed for trading. As a tool the theta provides:

1. for the premium writer, a measure to indicate the bet with the greatest time decay;

2. for the punter looking for gearing, the bet with the highest theta may well be the bet to avoid; while

3. for marketmakers, thetas provide the ability to hedge one bet with another in order to be theta neutral in front of, say, a long weekend.

Apart from these common features of thetas, binary thetas have little in common with conventional thetas. In particular they can take positive as well as negative values which can prove a major headache for the premium writer should the underlying travel through the strike so that writers who are expecting to take in premium now find they are paying out as the theta swings from negative to positive time decay.

Both binary and conventional theta are prone to the same increasing inaccuracy as time to expiry approaches zero. Nevertheless, they provide an essential parameter provided the deficiencies are clearly understood.

2.10 Exercises

1. Is the theta for the following prices of upbets and downbets positive or negative?

	Bet	Price
a	Upbet	65
b	Upbet	49
c	Downbet	50
d	Downbet	65

2. If the underlying is $50 and the theta of the $49 strike downbet is –5.1, roughly what will the theta of the $51 strike downbet be?

3. If there are eight days to expiry and one attempts to roughly approximate the time decay of a bet over the forthcoming single day, which theta would provide the most accurate estimate?

   a) the current 8-day theta

   b) the 7-day theta, or

   c) a theta somewhere in between the seventh and eighth day?

4. For each bet find the time decay over the requested number of days using the associated theta.

	No. of Day's Decay	Theta
Bet 1	1	5
Bet 2	2	5
Bet 3	5	10

5. The following table provides the prices of three bets at five separate points in time (t) where t–1 has one day less to expiry than t. Find an approximation to theta for each bet at time t.

	t+2	t+1	t	t–1	t–2
Bet 1	50.354	50.331	50.307	50.280	50.251
Bet 2	17.434	15.792	13.903	11.709	9.149
Bet 3	82.566	84.208	86.097	88.291	90.851

2.11 Answers

1. Thetas are negative when out-of-the-money, positive when in the money and zero when at-the-money. Therefore,

   a) Positive

   b) Negative

   c) Zero

   d) Positive

2. Since the $49 strike downbet and the $51 strike downbet are equidistant around the underlying they will have roughly the same absolute theta, i.e. 5.1. Therefore the $51 strike downbet will have a theta of roughly +5.1 since it is in the money and will therefore increase in value as time passes..

3. Both a) and b) provide average thetas at the single points of 8 days and 7 days to expiry exactly. The former will underestimate the one day time decay while the latter will overestimate it; therefore c) will provide the most accurate forecast.

4. Using the formula:

   Time Decay = 100 x (No. of Days x Theta) / 365

   Bet 1: 100 × ((1 × 5) / 365) = 1.37 points

   Bet 2: 100 × ((2 × 5) / 365) = 2.74 points

   Bet 3: 100 × ((5 × 10) / 365) = 13.70 points

5. Ignore t–2 and t+2, as the most accurate theta is obtained from making the increment in time as small as possible, i.e. as δt 0. Therefore subtracting the price at t+1 from the price at t–1 gives the difference in price over two days, and then multiplying by 365 and dividing by 100 provides the correct theta:

Theta $= [(P_{t-1} - P_{t+1}) / ((t + 1) - (t - 1))]*365/100$

Bet 1 $= [(50.280 - 50.331) / ((t + 1) - (t - 1))] \times 365 / 100 = -0.0931$

Bet 2 $= [(11.709 - 15.792) / ((t + 1) - (t - 1))] \times 365 / 100 = -7.4515$

Bet 3 $= [(88.291 - 84.208) / ((t + 1) - (t - 1))] \times 365 / 100 = 7.4515$

3

Vega & Volatility

3.0   Introduction

Vega is a ratio that measures how much the bet price will change due to a change in implied volatility.

All option pricing needs to make assumptions about the behaviour of certain variables. Some are clearly inappropriate, e.g. two of the main assumptions behind the Black-Scholes option-pricing model are that volatility remains a constant and that continuous hedging is feasible, both of which are plainly not true. But financial theorem in general often needs to make these assumptions in order to draw comparisons between one instrument and another for evaluation purposes. The gross redemption yield of a bond is a case in point. In calculating the g.r.y. there is an implicit assumption that all dividends will be reinvested in the same bond at the same gross redemption yield through to maturity. Totally unfeasible of course, but nevertheless the g.r.y. has provided one of the more enduring measures in the relative evaluation of bonds. By the same token, some of the underlying assumptions with respect to the pricing of stock, currency and bond options can also be considered a bit flaky and this chapter covers, possibly, the most tenuous of them all, volatility.

Volatility is a measure of the movement in the underlying. There are two measures of volatility, historic and implied. Historic volatility is a measure of past price movements, while implied is a number thrown out of the pricing algorithm if the option price is an input instead of volatility.

There will be no inclusion of Wiener processes or Brownian motions in this chapter so non-mathematicians need not bolt for the door just yet. An understanding of the normal and lognormal distribution would be an asset though.

3.1   Normal Distribution

Fig 3.1.1 illustrates two bell-shaped normal distributions. They are symmetrical about the mean, zero in this case, while the standard deviation, or volatility in options parlance, is 'low' or 'high'.

If the share price at any time is assumed to be the mean of the distribution, then the volatility measures the number of times the price has traded, or maybe settled, away from the mean. If readings were taken over a year measuring the difference in the price of a stock from one day to the next, then graphically the readings may be represented as a normal bell-shaped distribution. If the stock has low volatility then it would be expected that for a high number of incidences the stock will close at around the same price the following day. The frequency of the stock having a big move in one day will be rare and this distribution is reflected in the 'Low Volatility' graph. On the other hand if the stock is volatile then the incidence of a big move will be greater and the distribution will look more like the 'High Volatility' graph.

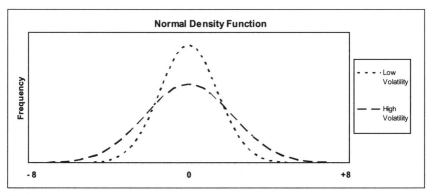

Figure 3.1.1

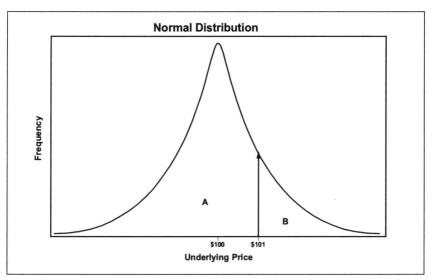

Figure 3.1.2

In Fig 3.1.2 the area under the graph and above the horizontal axis at zero frequency is 1, reflecting the total probability of an event taking place. In this illustration the arithmetic mean has been replaced by the current underlying price of $100 which is directly below the highest point of the distribution. If a vertical line was drawn from the peak to the horizontal axis then 50% of the total area would be to the left of this line and 50% to the right. This reflects the probability that there is a 50:50 chance of the underlying going up or down. To the right of $100 there is a vertical line at the strike price of $101. If the area B to the right of the $101 strike contains 40% of the total area A+B, then the probability of the underlying ending above the strike is 40% and it would be reasonable to expect the market price of the $101 upbet to be trading at 40.

If this normal distribution is an accurate fit of the movement of the underlying, then since the graph is symmetrical at about $100, the probability of the $99 downbet ending in-the-money, i.e. the underlying below $99, is also 40%.

3.2   Lognormal Distribution

There is a flaw with using the normal distribution for modelling the price movements of financial and commodity instruments and that is that absolute price movements are assumed. For example, if a healthy company has a share price trading at £1, should the probability of the share going down £1 be the same as the share going up £1? In effect, are the odds of the healthy company going bust with absolutely no assets producing a zero share price the same as the odds of the healthy company doubling the share price to £2? The answer is no, and in order to circumvent this problem, the lognormal distribution is used in financial engineering.

If the underlying moves from $100 to $80 then it has fallen 20%. If the underlying falls $20, from $120 to $100, then it has only fallen 16.667%. If the underlying falls from $125 to $100, then that is a 20% fall. In effect a distribution is required that gives a move from $100 down to $80 the same probability as a move from $100 up to $125. The lognormal distribution fits the bill since $-\log(\$80/\$100)=\log(\$125/\$100)$.

The lognormal distribution is shown in Fig 3.2.1 where there is a fatter skew to the right of the mean, so that when a lognormal distribution is used the $80 strike downbet is now worth less than the $120 strike upbet, reflecting a higher probability of an absolute move of $20 upwards rather than downwards.

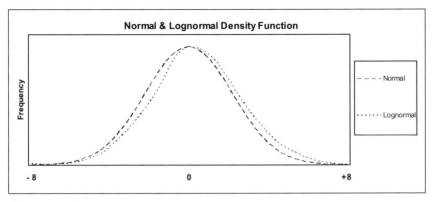

Figure 3.2.1

3.3 Historic Volatility & Implied Volatility

Historic volatility is a measurement derived from studying the past price behaviour of the underlying, while inputting the option price into the pricing model (instead of volatility) will generate the implied volatility.

Historic Volatility

The numbers required to calculate the 'fair value' of an option are the underlying price, the strike price, the time to expiry, volatility plus interest rates and yield (which are both assumed to be zero for the present in order to keep things simple). Since time to expiry, the current underlying price and the strike price are given, plus zero interest rates and yield are assumed, the volatility number in evaluating 'fair' value is the all important input. There are many statistical methods of calculating the historic volatility ranging from simple weighted averages through to more complicated stochastic methodologies. Many books have been written on this subject alone and this book is not going to compete in that space, but one observation can be made.

When assessing an accurate historic volatility for use in an options pricing, model the algorithm employed will generally be of less importance than the length of time used over each reading. For example, assume a trader wishes to trade a twenty-day option, should a 1-day, 20-day or 1-year moving average with respectively a 5%, 6% and 7% 'vol' be used? The twenty-day 'vol' would be the most appropriate because if the one-day 5% volatility is used then there is the ever-present danger of getting caught short when the market moves. Alternatively, the 7% one-year 'vol' could be too expensive since it is perfectly feasible that the market may be stagnant for 20 days and then become volatile for the remaining 232 trading days in the year.

'Scalpers' will take an ultra short-term view on 'vol' while funds look at the bigger picture adopting a range of various measures of stochastic volatilities. There is no such thing as the historic volatility but a myriad of techniques and timescales all deriving their own interpretation of historic volatility.

Implied Volatility

Implied volatility is the measure of standard deviation that is an output from Black-Scholes and other mathematical models available for evaluating options.

By entering the underlying, strike, time to expiry and option price one can generate the implied volatility. This volatility can then be used as the input to create a whole range of option prices for different strikes and underlying. With conventional options the preferable strike to use for calculating the implied volatility is the at-the-money option. This is because at-the-monies are generally more liquid so a keener price is available, but more importantly they have the most time value which is the factor on which volatility works. But with binary options the at-the-money is always 50 so it is necessary to generate two implied volatilities either side of the at-the-money and, bearing this in mind, the greatest liquidity will be found in an out-of-the-money upbet and out-of-the-money downbet.

Historic v Implied Volatility

An options marketmaker will always be bidding and offering around a volatility level where he feels the weight of options buying equates to the weight of options selling. To that end historical volatility is of little concern to him, just a constant assessment as to where the 'implied' is at any one time. Alternatively an options hedge fund may specialise in studying historic volatility in order to go 'long' or 'short' premium. The relative importance of historical and implied volatility is very much dependent on the trader's view on random walk theory and Chartism. If the reader is by nature a chartist then it is more likely that the historic volatility concept will weigh more heavily than fundamentals. Alternatively the fundamentalist is more likely to study the schedule of upcoming announcements on economic data and events and attempt to gauge what kind of reaction they are likely to precipitate in the marketplace.

A brief anecdote might better describe the gulf that can occur between the two separate views of volatility. In 1992 the author was trading conventional options on 90-day Sterling LIBOR futures. The future was trading at 89.25 with the 89.00 Puts on offer at 1 tick a thousand contracts. The options had two and a half days to go to expiry. The implied volatility of the 89.00 Puts was about 14.8% with the at-the-money 89.25 straddle trading at around 12%. On the (arguable) assumption that the straddle was a more accurate reflection of historic volatility than the 89.00 Put, even at 1 tick the 89.00 Puts looked expensive with an implied volatility of 14.8%. An associate bought the thousand on offer. Two days later sterling came under such pressure that the UK government was forced to raise interest rates by 2% to 12% leading to the future expiring that day at 88.00 with the 89.00 Puts expiring worth 100. The trader who bought the 89.00 Puts grossed £1.25m on a £12,500 outlay. Basically the implied 'vol' was too cheap and was not accurately reflecting the tumult that was going to occur in the next two days. Implied volatility is important, so too is historic volatility, but what is most important is forecasting where historic volatility is going to be because that is where the real money is.

3.4   Upbets v the Underlying as a function of Volatility

An increase in implied volatility increases the price of conventional options. Nothing so regimented can be ascribed to binaries. Fig 3.4.1 illustrates upbet price profiles with five days to expiry, a strike price of $100 and implied volatilities as per the legend. The out-of-the-money upbets (where the underlying is lower than $100) increase in value as the 'vol' increases from 1% to 9% but, when in-the-money, the upbets decrease in value over the same increase in 'vol'.

The price of an upbet is the probability of the underlying being above the strike at some time in the future, so if the underlying is trading at $99.70 and volatility falls there is less chance of the underlying rising to travel through $100. Correspondingly, if the upbet is in-the-money then the converse applies with, a winning upbet likely to have a better chance of

50

remaining a winning bet if volatility falls as there is less chance of the underlying falling out-of-the-money.

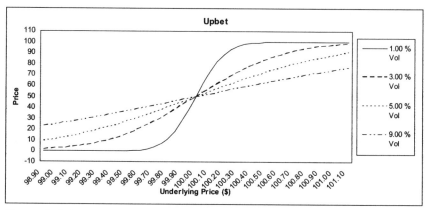

Figure 3.4.1

Clearly changes in volatility affect upbet prices in a similar way to time decay.

3.5   Vega and the Impact of Volatility

In Fig 3.4.1 if a vertical line were drawn at the underlying of 99.70 and instead of just the four volatilities plotted from 1% to 9% there were volatilities plotted from 2.5% to 45% then the second graph from the top in Fig 3.5.1 would plot the relationship between the bet price and volatility.

The gradient at any point on the graph is the vega and is denoted by:

$$V = \delta P / \delta \sigma$$

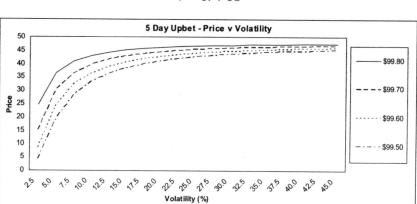

Figure 3.5.1

where: P   =   price of the option, and

         σ   =   implied volatility

leading to δP =   a change in the price

and $\delta\sigma$ =   a change in implied volatility.

Vega therefore measures the ratio of a change in the bet price brought about by a change in implied volatility.

	Implied Volatility						
	5.0%	7.5%	10.0%	12.5%	15.0%	17.5%	20.0%
				Gradient			
$\delta\sigma = 0$				0.6179			
$\delta\sigma = 2.5$			39.64	0.6440	42.86		
$\delta\sigma = 5.0$		36.44		0.7330		43.77	
$\delta\sigma = 7.5$	30.28			0.9433			44.43

Table 3.5.1

Table 3.5.1 displays the prices of upbets with the underlying at $99.70 and the implied volatility ranging from 5% to 20% with five days to expiry. In the 12.50% column the gradient of the curve can be seen to approach the vega as the incremental changes decrease from $\delta\sigma = 7.5\%$ to $\delta\sigma = 0$, the vega being reached at $\delta\sigma = 0$, i.e. 0.6179, which is the slope of the tangent to the curve at 12.5%.

The gradient is calculated by the following formula:

Gradient   = $(P_2 - P_1) / (\sigma_2 - \sigma_1)$

where P_2 =   higher bet price

        P_1 =   lower bet price

        σ_2 =   higher implied volatility

        σ_1 =   lower implied volatility

so that at $\delta\sigma = 5.0$,

Gradient   = $(43.77 - 36.44) / (17.5 - 7.5)$

           =   0.7330.

A further point of note is that, as opposed to the theta where the tangents were all negative (except in extreme time), here the tangents are all positive indicating that an increase in implied volatility for an out-of-the-money upbet will always increase the value of the bet.

3.6 Upbet Vega

Vega measures the slopes of the curve in Fig 3.5.1 and is and indication of how much the upbet will change in value for a 1% move in implied volatility.

	Underlying Price				
	$99.50	$99.60	$99.70	$99.80	$99.90
5 Days	4.7076	4.2951	3.5648	2.5499	1.3206
10 Days	3.9852	3.4003	2.6769	1.8405	0.9243

Table 3.6.1

Table 3.6.1 lists vegas for 5 and 10-day upbets based on a 5% implied volatility. For example, with 5 days to expiry and the underlying at $99.50, the $100.00 upbet has a fair value of 19.50 and a vega of 4.7076. If 'vol' falls to 4% or rises to 6%, what will the upbet be worth? The formula is:

$$P_1 \;=\; P_0 + (\sigma_1 - \sigma_0) \times V$$

where P_1 =   new upbet price

P_0 =   original upbet price

σ_1 =   new implied volatility

σ_0 =   original implied volatility

and V =   vega

So that at 4%   Upbet = 19.50 + (4 − 5) × 4.7076 = 14.7924

and at 6%   Upbet = 19.50 + (6 − 5) × 4.7076 = 24.2076

The fair values at 4% and 6% are actually 14.16 and 23.66 respectively, so the vega is out by 4.47% and just 2.26%, which is accurate enough for most risk analysis. If values at 4.5% and 5.5% volatilities are required, then the accuracy would be even greater as the closer the 'vol' is to the current 'vol' the more accurate the results.

Vega is a crucial 'greek' for option marketmakers who are constantly looking to neutralise their book against movements in implied volatility. Fig 3.6.1 illustrates vegas for 5-day upbets with a $100 strike and the 'vols' listed in the legend.

Points of note are:

1. The profiles intersect when at-the-money since the upbet will always be worth 50 irrespective of the 'vol', therefore vega is zero for every profile.

2. The profiles also intersect away from the strike. The 3% profile intersects with the 9% profile three times in total, thoroughly unlike the behaviour of conventional options.

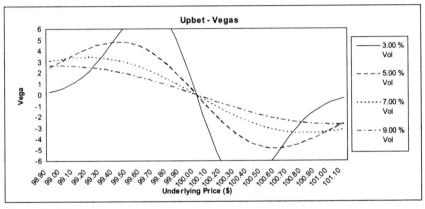

Figure 3.6.1

3. The highest and lowest vega of each profile approach the strike as volatility progressively falls.

3.7 Downbets & Volatility

Fig 3.7.1 illustrates four profiles for a one-year downbet with a strike of $100 and implied volatilities as per the legend. As the volatility rises from 1% to 25% the out-of-the-money downbets with the underlying greater than $100 rise in value while the in-the-monies fall in value. At the underlying price of $96 the 1% to 25% downbets are respectively 100, 85.10, 65.55 and 61.34 reflecting the probability that with the downbet $4 in-the-money and volatility only 1%, there is no chance that the underlying will be above $100 in one year's time. As the underlying becomes more volatile and the implied volatility rises to 25% the probability of the underlying remaining below $100 in a year's time has fallen to 58.7%. The reverse logic applies to the out-of-the-monies.

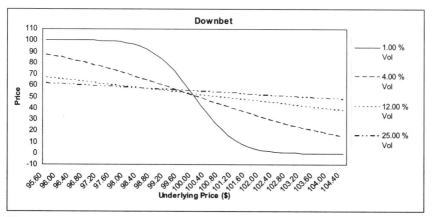

Figure 3.7.1

At the underlying of $96 there is very little difference in price between the 12% and 25% downbet prices indicating a very low absolute vega, compared to the gap between the 4% and 1% prices indicating a high vega.

3.8 Downbet Vega

The vegas of Fig 3.8.1 relate to the price profiles of Fig 3.7.1.

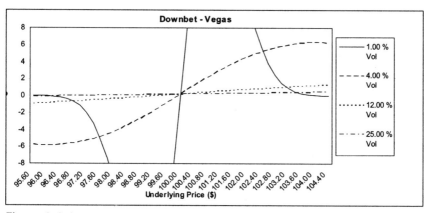

Figure 3.8.1

The 25% price profile translates to an almost flat zero vega while the 12% vega barely deviates more. The 4% vega tops out at around the absolute level of 6% whereas the 1% vega disappears from the graph. The 1% vega actually reaches ±24, which lacks credibility as the at-the-money is worth 50, so the out-of-the-money downbet must be within the range 0–50. According to the vega of +24 this downbet would only need a fall or rise of 1% to cover pretty much the whole trading range available. The vega of 24 is only accurate for a very localised area on the graph, and therefore yet again it is vital to understand the limitations of the 'greeks' and not take the sensitivity analysis presented at face value.

3.9   Vega & Extreme Implied Volatility

Fig 3.9.1 illustrates upbet values plotted against implied volatilities with the underlying being as indicated in the legend, with the strike $100 and 5 days to expiry. It is Fig 3.5.1 with a much wider range of volatility extending up to 180%.

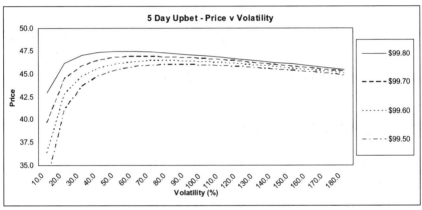

Figure 3.9.1

What is evident from the graph is that as the volatility increases from 10% there is a maximum upbet value beyond which the upbet starts to fall in value. This peculiarity exists for similar reasons to the non-monotonic characteristic of the theta discussed in Section 2.6. At an underlying of $99.50 the upbet is 50¢ out-of- the-money and the effect from an increase in volatility has only limited impact on the bet price, which is now influenced far more by the movement in the underlying. As volatility increases, since the upbet price is constrained on the upside by the limit of 50, an increase in volatility tends to focus more on the probability of the underlying falling, so adversely effecting the value of the upbet.

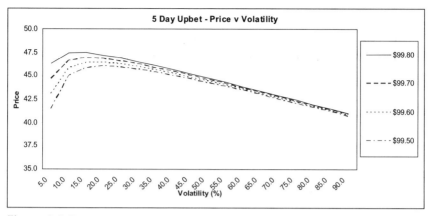

Figure 3.9.2

Fig 3.9.2 illustrates how an excessively high implied volatility aligned with three months to expiry provides quite a steep decline in the upbet price from its peak. Increasing both time to expiry plus implied volatility increases the rate of decline of the value of the upbet.

A practical problem created as a side effect is that when calculating the implied volatility from current market prices one can always provide two separate answers. When considering the $99.50 profile in Fig 3.9.2 an upbet price of 45 can produce implied volatilities of 10% and 40%, which could well provide an absolute error in implied volatility of 30%. Using the incorrect implied volatility to subsequently evaluate other bets in the series will provide disastrous evaluations and severe financial loss.

Clearly the same scenario could impact on the price of not just out-of-the-money upbets but also out-of-the-money downbets, but it should be stressed that the likelihood of such a situation as Fig 3.9.2 actually existing is remote since any savvy trader will take advantage of the situation and in the above case sell the hedged upbet. If the volatility moves up or down the position will generate a profit. The volatility at the peak of the $99.50 profile is at 20% and this level of volatility will almost assuredly have been approached from below since sellers of out-of-the-money upbets, or volatility, will know that the upbet has an upside limit of 45, therefore a volatility above 20% will never be reached.

3.10 Bets v Conventionals

Fig 3.10.1 illustrates upbet and downbet vegas in comparison to conventional call and put vegas.

The points of note are:

1. The call vega is the same as the put vega whereas upbet and downbet vegas are mirror-images of each other through the horizontal axis.

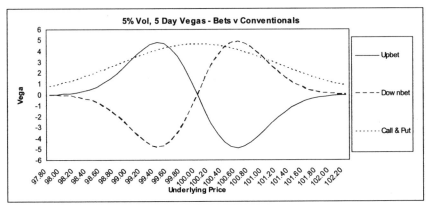

Figure 3.10.1

2. Upbet and downbet vegas can be either positive or negative whereas the conventional vega is always positive.

3. At-the-money upbet and downbet vegas are zero whereas conventional vegas are at their highest.

3.11 Formulae

Upbet/Binary Call Vega $\quad = -e^{-rt}\, N'(d_2)\,(\sqrt{t} + \tfrac{d_2}{\sigma})$

Downbet/Binary Put Vega $\quad = -e^{-rt}\, N'(d_2)\,(\sqrt{t} + \tfrac{d_2}{\sigma})$

where $\quad = d_2 = \dfrac{\log(\tfrac{S}{E}) + (r - D - \tfrac{1}{2}\sigma^2)t}{\sigma\sqrt{t}}$

$$N'(x) = \dfrac{1}{\sqrt{2\pi}}\, e^{-0.5x^2}$$

and
S = price of the underlying

E = strike/exercise price

r = risk free rate of interest

D = continuous dividend yield of underlying

$$t \ = \ \text{time in years to expiry}$$

$$\sigma \ = \ \text{annualised standard deviation of asset returns}$$

3.12 Summary

Of all the inputs in options evaluation the implied volatility is the most critical. Time to expiry, the underlying price and the strike are all given, while the volatility requires an assessment by the trader. Being able to intuitively understand where volatility should be is very often the difference between an average and a very good options trader. But pricing the option correctly is one thing, understanding how changes in volatility then affect the options price is another, and when running an options book understanding vega is just as important as getting the bet on at the right price.

3.13 Exercises

1. Is the vega for the following upbets and downbets positive or negative?

	Bet	Price
a	Upbet	65
b	Upbet	49
c	Downbet	50
d	Downbet	72

2. A short position in an out-of-the-money downbet is a long vega position. True or False?

3. A long position in a downbet trading at 60 will be profitable if implied volatility rises. True or False?

4. If the underlying is $100 and the vega of the $99 strike downbet is 5.1, approximately what will the vega of the $101 strike upbet be?

5. To gain exposure to a forecast rise in the volatility (actual, not implied) of the underlying one should:

   a) Sell out-of-the-money upbets

   b) Buy in-the-money upbets

c) Sell in-the-money downbets

d) Buy out-of-the-money downbets

prior to trading futures to become delta neutral.

6. The following table provides bets with prices and vegas. The last column shows the change in volatility. What will the bets be worth once the change in implied volatility comes into effect?

		Price	Vega	Change in Implied Volatility
a	Upbet	37.3	4.42	+1%
b	Upbet	68.9	−2.74	−0.4%
c	Downbet	27.2	1.89	−0.8%

N.B. A change of +1% indicates a change from 4% Vol to 5% Vol for instance.

3.14 Answers

1. a) Negative. The upbet with a price of 65 is in-the-money so an increase in implied volatility is more likely to push the bet out-of-the-money therefore the bet falls in value.

   b) Positive. This upbet is slightly out-of-the-money so an increase in implied volatility will increase its chance of winning.

   c) Zero. Irrespective of volatility the at-the-money bet is always worth 50, impervious to changes in implied volatility, and therefore has a zero vega.

   d) Negative. The downbet is worth 72 and therefore in-the-money and has a negative vega.

2. False. An out-of-the-money downbet has a positive vega as an increase in implied volatility increases the bet's chance of being a winner. Therefore a short out-of-the-money position is a negative vega position.

3. False. Any bet trading at 60 is in-the-money. If implied volatility rises the in-the-money bet will lose value so the long downbet with a price of 60 will incur a loss if implied volatility rises.

4. Both the $99 strike downbet and the $101 strike upbet are $1 out-of-the-money. Therefore the $101 upbet will have the same vega as the $99 downbet, i.e. approx 5.1.

5. If the trader takes the view that volatility will rise then they should be getting long gammas. To achieve this the trader should sell in-the-money bets and buy out-of-the-money bets. Therefore c) and d) are correct.

6. New price = Old price + (V * change in Implied Vol)

    a) New Price   =   37.3 + (4.42 × 1)

                 =   41.72

    b) New Price   =   68.9 + (−2.74 × −0.4)

                 =   69.97

    c) New Price   =   27.2 + (1.89 × −0.8)

                 =   25.69

4

Delta & Underlying

4.0   Introduction

Delta is a ratio that measures how much the bet price will change owing to a change in the underlying.

Of all the 'greeks' the delta is probably the most utilised amongst traders. The delta is the gradient of the slope of the binary options price profile versus the underlying, and measures the exposure of the option to a movement in the underlying. The attraction of the delta as a meaningful number is that the delta translates bets, whether single bets or a portfolio of bets, into an equivalent position of a tradeable entity, i.e. the underlying. An upbet with a delta of 0.5 means that if, for instance, a share price goes up 1¢, then the upbet will increase in value by ½¢. Alternatively, a long 100 T-Note upbet position with a delta of 0.5 has an incidental P&L equivalent to being long 50 T-Note futures.

This section focuses on the behaviour of the binary delta and finally draws comparisons with the delta of the conventional option.

4.1   Deltas and the Gradient of the Price Profile

The delta of any option is defined by:

$$\Delta = \delta P / \delta S$$

where: P   =   price of the option, and

S   =   price of the underlying

so that δS =   a change in the value of S

and δP =   a change in the value of P.

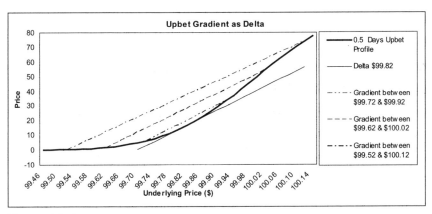

Figure 4.1.1

65

The delta is therefore the ratio of the change in price of the option given a change in the price of the underlying.

To explain this concept the 0.5 days upbet profile in Fig 4.1.1 is extracted from the 0.5 day curve in Fig 2.1.1 between the underlying of $99.46 and $100.14. It is possible to approximate deltas from the upbet prices either side of the underlying (S) at which one wants to calculate the delta. The formula is:

Gradient $=$ $(P_2 - P_1) / (S_2 - S_1)$

where S_2 $=$ $S + \delta S$

S_1 $=$ $S - \delta S$

P_2 $=$ Bet value at S_2

P_1 $=$ Bet value at S_1

	$99.52	$99.62	$99.72	$99.82	$99.92	$100.02	$100.12
				Gradient			
$\delta S = 0$				1.3433			
$\delta S = 10$¢			6.4749	1.3381	33.2364		
$\delta S = 20$¢		1.9783		1.3072		54.266	
$\delta S = 30$¢	0.4648			1.2276			74.1226

Table 4.1.1

Table 4.1.1 provides the upbet prices at the underlying of $99.52 to $100.12 with the gradient sitting in the S = $99.82 column. The gradient at $\delta S = 30$¢ is:

Gradient $=$ $(74.1226 - 0.4648) / (100 \times (\$100.12 - \$99.52))$

$=$ 1.2276

N.B. The denominator ($S_2 - S_1$) needs to be multiplied by 100 since the minimum price movement is 0.01.

As the price difference narrows (as reflected by $\delta S = 20$¢ and $\delta S = 10$¢) the gradient tends to the delta of 1.3433. The delta is therefore the first differential of the bet price with respect to the underlying and can be stated mathematically as:

$$\text{as } \delta S \quad , \quad \Delta = dP / dS$$

which means that as δS falls to zero the gradient approaches the tangent (delta) of the price profile of Fig 4.1.1.

4.2 Upbet Deltas

Fig 4.2.1 illustrates deltas for a five-day upbet with a strike price of $100 and volatilities as in the legend and are derived from the upbet price profiles of Fig 3.4.1.

The first point of note is that for the same volatility, the delta of the upbet which is 50 ticks in-the-money is the same as the delta of the upbet 50 ticks out-of-the-money. In other words the deltas are horizontally symmetric about the underlying when at-the-money, i.e. when the underlying is at $100.

In Fig 3.4.1 the 9% profile is fairly shallow in comparison to the other three profiles. From the 9% delta in Fig 4.2.1 the gradient of the 9% profile in Fig 3.4.1 can be seen to fluctuate between 25%-30%. In Fig 3.4.1, with the volatility at 1% and the underlying below $100, there is little chance of the upbet being a winning bet until the underlying gets close to the strike, where the price profile steepens sharply to travel up through 0.5 before levelling out short of the upbet price of 100. The 1% delta in Fig 4.2.1 reflects this dramatic change of upbet price with the 1% delta profile showing zero delta followed by a sharply increasing delta as the upbet price changes dramatically over a small change in the underlying, followed by a sharply decreasing delta as the delta reverts to zero as the upbet levels off at the higher price.

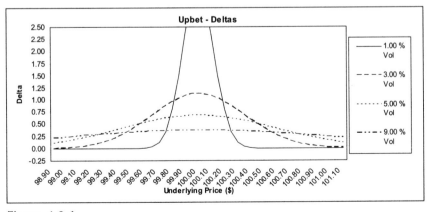

Figure 4.2.1

From Fig 3.4.1 the upbet price profile always has a positive slope so the upbet deltas are always positive.

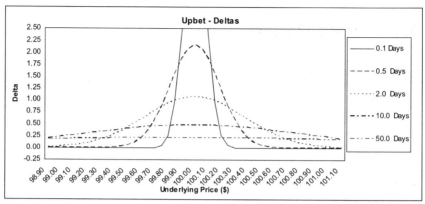

Figure 4.2.2

Earlier it was mentioned that decreasing volatility and time to expiry have a similar impact on the price of an option. Fig 4.2.2 defines deltas as time to expiry decreases and indeed, the graph is very similar to Fig 4.2.1.

What is worth noting in Fig 4.2.2 is the extreme steepling of the delta as time falls to 0.1 day to expiry. From 2 days to expiry the at-the-money upbet has a delta of 1.08, increasing to 2.16 with 0.5 day to expiry, and then subsequently 4.82 with 0.1 day to expiry. This is very much in contrast with a conventional option delta where the absolute value of the delta cannot exceed 1. Furthermore, in this chapter's introduction the trader 'long' 100 at-the-money T-Note upbets now with 0.1 day to expiry finds that he is now long an equivalent 482 futures. This is extreme gearing!

	Underlying Price				
	$99.60	$99.65	$99.70	$99.75	$99.80
Price	31.2623	33.4403	35.6745	37.9577	40.2825
Delta	0.4296	0.4414	0.4520	0.4611	0.4686

Table 4.2.1

Table 4.2.1 shows 10 day, 5% volatility upbet prices with deltas. At $99.65 the upbet is worth 33.4403 and has a delta of 0.4414. Therefore, if the underlying rises one tick from $99.65 to $99.66 the upbet will rise in value 0.4414 from 33.4403 to 33.8817. Likewise, if the underlying rises from $99.65 to $99.70 the upbet at $99.70 will be worth:

$$33.4403 + 5 \times 0.4414 = 35.6473$$

while if the underlying fell 5 ticks to $99.60 the upbet would be worth:

$$33.4403 + (-5) \times 0.4414 = 31.2333.$$

At $99.70 and $99.60 the upbet value in Table 4.2.1 is 35.6745 and 31.2623 so there is a slight discrepancy between the values calculated above and true values in the table. This is because the delta of 0.4414 is the delta for just the one underlying level of $99.65. At $99.70 and $99.60 the deltas are 0.4520 and 0.4296 respectively so the value of 0.4414 is too low when assessing the upward move, but overstates the change in upbet price when the underlying falls. If the average of the two deltas at $99.65 and $99.70 is (0.4414 + 0.4520) / 2 = 0.4467 and this number is used in the above calculation, the upbet at $99.70 would be estimated as:

$$33.4403 + 5 \times 0.4467 = 35.6738$$

an error of 0.0007. The average delta between $99.60 and $99.65 is:

$$(0.4296 + 0.4414) / 2 = 0.4355.$$

The price at $99.60 would now be assessed as:

$$33.4403 + (-5 \times 0.4355) = 31.2628$$

an error of just 0.0005. The next chapter on gamma will provide the answers as to why this discrepancy exists.

4.3 Downbet Deltas

Downbet deltas are always negative or zero and like the upbet deltas are symmetrical about the at-the-money underlying price. Downbet deltas are also symmetrical with upbet deltas through the horizontal axis, providing the volatility and time to expiry are the same. Fig 4.3.1 illustrates downbet deltas with 25 days to expiry and volatility as in the legend while Fig 4.3.2 illustrates downbet deltas with volatility of 25% and time to expiry as in the legend.

The delta of the downbet with 25 days to expiry and 25% volatility is approximately −0.07 across the whole range of the underlying. This suggests that the downbet price profile is almost a straight line with a very shallow gradient which indicates the underlying has very little impact on the downbet price. The downbet at an underlying of $99.00 is 57.3904 so over the $1 move in the underlying from $100 to $99 the delta on average is:

$$(50.0 - 57.3904) / 100 = -0.0739$$

indicating that the downbet increases in value by only 0.0739 tick for every one point move down in the underlying.

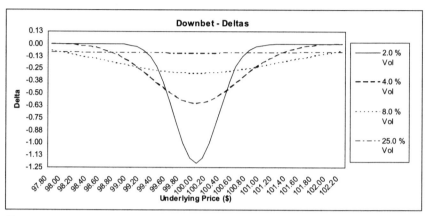

Figure 4.3.1

Fig 4.3.2 has a similar shape to Fig 4.3.1 but take a closer look at the legends and the scale on the axes.

		Underlying Price			
	$99.98	$99.99	$100.00	$100.01	$100.02
0.00001	−0.0008	−5.1984	−96.4088	−5.2009	−0.0008
0.001	−8.5788	−9.3639	−9.6409	−9.3630	−8.5774

Table 4.3.1

Table 4.3.1 provides the downbet deltas for 0.00001 and 0.001 days to expiry which equate to the 5.3 minutes and 8.8 hours respectively in the legend of Fig 4.3.2. In the last five minutes the absolute delta of the at-the-money $100 downbet exceeds 100 and indeed approaches infinity as the time to expiry approaches zero. Clearly yet again this is a mathematical anomaly because in practice the delta could not exceed 100 since the at-the-money downbet with a price of 50 can in fact only change value by ±50.

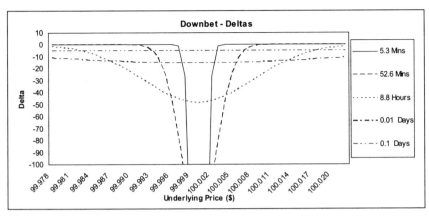

Figure 4.3.2

Once again the trader must be very wary of taking 'greeks' at face value as expiry becomes imminent.

4.4   Bets v Conventionals

Fig 4.4.1 provides a comparison of upbet, downbet and conventional call and put deltas.

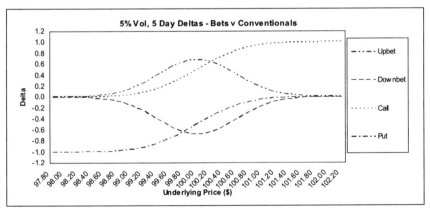

Figure 4.4.1

Points of note are:

1. Downbet and upbet deltas mirror each other through the horizontal axis.

2. Whereas the call and put deltas are constrained to an absolute value of 0.5 when the option is at-the-money, the upbet and downbet deltas

are at their absolute highest when at-the-money and have no constraint being able to approach infinity as time to expiry approaches zero.

3. The call delta profile resembles the price of the upbet while the put delta profile resembles the price of the downbet multiplied by -1.

4.5 Formulae

Downbet/Binary Put Delta $\quad = \dfrac{e^{-rt}\, N'(d_2)}{\sigma S \sqrt{t}}$

Downbet/Binary Put Delta $\quad = \dfrac{-\,e^{-rt}\, N'(d_2)}{\sigma S \sqrt{t}}$

where $\quad = d_2 = \dfrac{\log(\frac{S}{E}) + (r - D - \frac{1}{2}\sigma^2)t}{\sigma\sqrt{t}}$

$$N'(x) = \frac{1}{\sqrt{2\pi}}\, e^{-0.5x^2}$$

and

S = price of the underlying

E = strike/exercise price

r = risk free rate of interest

D = continuous dividend yield of underlying

t = time in years to expiry

σ = annualised standard deviation of asset returns

4.6 Summary

Deltas provide instant and easily understood information on the behaviour of the price of a bet in relation to a change in the underlying. Upbets always have positive deltas and downbets have negative deltas so an increase in the underlying causes an increase in the value of the upbet and a decrease in the value of the downbet.

When a trader takes a position in any bet they are immediately exposed to possible adverse movements in time, volatility and the underlying. The risk of the latter can be immediately negated by taking an opposite position in the underlying equivalent to the delta of the position. For bookrunners and marketmakers hedging against an adverse movement in the underlying is of prime importance and hence the delta is the most widely used of the 'greeks'.

Nevertheless, as expiry approaches the delta can reach ludicrously high numbers so one should always observe the tenet: "Beware Greeks bearing silly analysis numbers…".

4.7 Exercises

1. The same strike, same expiry upbet and downbet deltas always sum to 1. True or False?

2. To gain exposure to a forecast rise in the underlying one should:
   a) Sell upbets
   b) Buy upbets
   c) Sell downbets
   d) Buy downbets

3. The strike with the highest absolute delta is:
   a) the strike most in-the-money
   b) the strike most out-of-the-money
   c) the strike nearest the underlying
   d) the strike with the highest implied volatility
   e) the strike with the lowest implied volatility

4. The price of an upbet and downbet with the underlying are provided in the following table. What is the best approximation of the delta at an underlying of $99.70, $99.90, $100.10 and $100.30?

	99.6	99.8	100	100.2	100.4
Upbet Price	25.2	37.1	50.0	63.0	75.0
Downbet Price	74.8	62.9	50.0	37.0	25.0

5. In Question 4, assuming the delta changes in a constant manner what would the price of an upbet be at the underlying of $100.60?

4.8 Answers

1. False. The downbet delta is the upbet delta reflected through the horizontal axis, therefore the downbet delta is the negative of the upbet delta and subsequently upbet and downbet deltas always sum to zero.

2. Upbets have a positive delta, downbets negative. Buying upbets generates positive deltas and selling upbets generates negative deltas, and vice versa for downbets. Therefore b) and c) provide upside exposure.

3. For starters d) and e) are irrelevant and have no bearing on the issue whatsoever. A conventional option with the strike most in-the-money or out-of-the-money will have the highest and lowest absolute delta respectively but this does not apply to binaries. The bet with the highest delta will be the at-the-money where the delta can approach infinity an instant prior to expiry. c) is the correct answer.

4. Upbet:

    $99.70 Δ = (37.1 − 25.2) / [($99.80 − $99.60) × 100]

              = 0.595

    $99.90 Δ = (50.0 − 37.1) / [($100.00 − $99.80) × 100]

              = 0.645

    $100.10 Δ = (63.0 − 50.0) / [($100.20 − $100.00) × 100]

              = 0.65

    $100.30 Δ = (75.0 − 63.0) / [($100.40 − $100.20) × 100]

              = 0.6

    Downbet:

    $99.70 Δ = (60.9 − 71.4) / [($99.80 − $99.60) × 100]

              = − 0.525

    $99.90 Δ = (50.0 − 60.9) / [($100.00 − $99.80) × 100]

              = − 0.545

$100.10 Δ = (39.0 − 50.0) / [($100.20 − $100.00) × 100]

= − 0.55

$100.30 Δ = (29.0 − 39.0) / [($100.40 − $100.20) × 100]

= − 0.5

5. The delta at $100.10 is 0.65 and at $100.30 is 0.6, a fall of 0.05. A constant change in delta would therefore imply that the delta at $100.50 would be 0.55.

The upbet price can then be extracted from the equation:

0.55 = (Upbet − 75.0) / [($100.60 − $100.40) × 100]

and rearranging:

Upbet − 75.0 = 0.55 × [($100.60 - $100.40) × 100]

= 11.0

therefore:

Upbet = 11.0 + 75.0 = 86.0

5

Gamma & Delta

5.0   Introduction

Gamma is a ratio that measures how much the delta will change owing to a change in the underlying.

The gamma is the measure most commonly used by marketmakers or 'structural' traders when referring to portfolios of options. The gamma indicates how much the delta of an option or portfolio of options will change over a one-point move.

Marketmakers will generally try to hold books that are neutral to movements in the underlying, but will more often than not be a long or a short gamma player. The long or short gamma indicates the position's exposure to swings in the delta and therefore subsequent exposure to the underlying. Gamma provides a very quick, one glance assessment of the position with respect to a change in the underlying and the delta so is subsequently a very important tool to the binary portfolio risk manager.

5.1   Gamma and the Gradient of the Delta

The gamma Γ of a binary option is defined by:

$$\Gamma = \delta\Delta \, / \, \delta S$$

where: Δ =   the delta of the bet

   S =   price of the underlying

so that δS =   a change in the value of the underlying

and $\delta\Delta$ =   a change in the value of the delta.

The gamma is therefore the ratio of the change in the option delta given a change in the price of the underlying. Furthermore, since the delta is the first derivative of a change in the bet price with respect to a change in the underlying it follows that the gamma is the second derivative of a change in the bet price with respect to a change in the underlying. So the equation of the gamma can also be written as:

$$\Gamma = \delta^2 P \, / \, \delta S^2$$

where: P =   the price of the upbet.

Fig 5.1.1 is a section of Fig 4.2.2 displaying the 2-day delta along with the tangent at \$100.12. The tangent has a gradient of –0.8989 and reflects the fact that this upbet is in-the-money with the delta falling from its peak of 1.0799 when at-the-money to 1.0221 at $100.12. The gradient of the tangent at $100.12 is the gamma which is negative and reflects that the upbet price profile is flattening out.

By substituting the delta for price in the equation to calculate the deltas in Section 4.1, one gets to the following equation to calculate the gamma:

$$\text{Gamma} = (\Delta_2 - \Delta_1) / (S_2 - S_1)$$

where
$$S_2 = S + \delta S$$
$$S_1 = S - \delta S$$
$$\Delta_2 = \text{delta at } S_2$$
$$\Delta_1 = \text{delta at } S_1$$

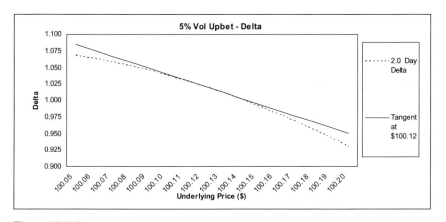

Figure 5.1.1

Table 5.1.1 is Table 4.2.1 with gammas added.

	Underlying Price				
	$99.60	$99.65	$99.70	$99.75	$99.80
Price	31.2623	33.4403	35.6745	37.9577	40.2825
Delta	0.4296	0.4414	0.4520	0.4611	0.4686
Gamma	0.2505	0.2245	0.1966	0.1666	0.1349

Table 5.1.1

In Section 4.2, in attempting to approximate the price of the upbet at $99.60 the average delta between the underlying at $99.60 to $99.65 was calculated and subtracted from the price at $99.65. At $99.60 the upbet was calculated as 31.2333, which generated an error of 0.029. This discrepancy was explained by the fact that the delta does not move from 0.4414 to 0.4296 in a straight line.

The gamma itself can then be used as the tool by which to assess what the delta will be in almost exactly the same way that the delta can be used to assess what the bet price will be. The average gamma between $99.65 and $99.70 is:

$$\text{Gamma} \quad = \quad (0.2245 + 0.1966) / (2 \times 100)$$
$$= \quad 0.0021055$$

N.B. In this instance the numerator is divided by 100 since the gamma is a measure over the underlying moving 1.0, while this example required the gamma over price increments of 0.01.

The delta at $99.65 can then be estimated by:

$$\text{Delta} \quad = \quad 0.4520 - (0.0021055 \times 5)$$
$$= \quad 0.4415$$

The delta is out by 0.0001 and this itself can be explained by the fact that the gamma does not move linearly itself.

The use of gamma as a tool is explored at length in the chapter on Hedging.

5.2 Upbet Gamma

The profile of $100 strike upbet gammas with 5% volatility are displayed in Fig 5.2.1. The gamma is always positive when the underlying is below the strike and negative above the strike, while at-the-money the gamma is always zero.

As illustrated in Fig 4.2.2 the closer the upbet to expiry the steeper the slopes of the delta so that as time passes the peak and trough of the gamma travel towards the at-the-money strike. The 50-day upbet had a delta that stayed within the bounds of 0.18 and 0.22, which is illustrated in Fig 5.2.1 by a gamma of almost zero for upbets with 50 days to expiry but increasingly high gammas as the days to expiry decrease.

A pertinent point for delta neutral traders is that what may be a positive (long) gamma position one moment can change to a negative (short) gamma position the next. This can be of vital importance to the marketmaker who may have 'taken his eye off' his position having assumed that being long gamma the position will look after itself, only to find that the underlying has travelled through a strike and the consequent change in deltas has handed him a losing position.

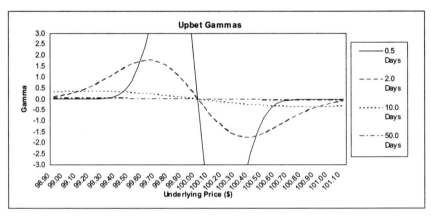

Figure 5.2.1

Fig 5.2.2 illustrates 5-day upbet gammas over changes in implied volatility. A reduction in time to expiry once again has a similar effect to implied volatility falling. In the instance of volatility, at 1% the gamma can switch from +17.29 to −17.26 in just a forty tick move from $99.80 to $100.20. Yet again delta neutral traders would have a torrid time risk managing such a book and the only consolation would be that at 1% volatility it is highly unlikely that the underlying would move at all thereby eliminating the need to hedge a losing book.

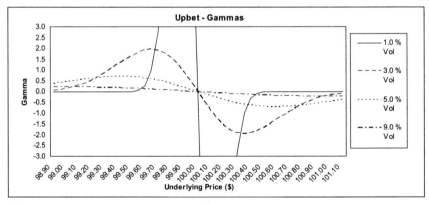

Figure 5.2.2

5.3 Downbet Gamma

The downbet gamma is the negative of the same strike upbet gamma therefore the gamma is positive when the underlying is above the strike and negative when below, corresponding to the downbet being out-of and in-the-money respectively.

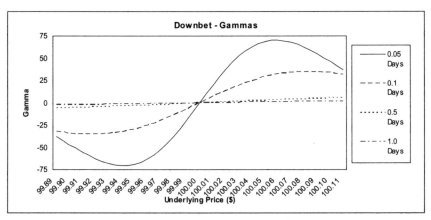

Figure 5.3.1

The profile of $100 strike downbet gammas with 5% volatility are displayed in Fig 5.3.1. The legend indicates very small times to expiry, while the underlying range is very narrow. This combination necessitates the left-hand scale running from ±75.

	Underlying Price				
	$99.98	$99.985	$99.99	$99.995	$100.00
52.6min	0.0	0.0	-150	-17.940	0.8
8.8 hrs	−759	−2,043	−3,392	−2,932	0.2

Table 5.3.1

Table 5.3.1 provides gammas that would pertain to Fig 4.3.2 which, as expiry approaches, have become totally worthless as analytical risk-management tools. Indeed with an underlying of $99.995 and 52.6 minutes to expiry the gamma is −17,940. The problem with these numbers are not that they're erroneous, but the fact that they are accurate for that exact underlying. At $99.99, just a half tick lower, the gamma is just [sic] −150 and half a tick higher just 0.8. The upshot is that if the trader wants to trade delta neutral then avoid these instruments at expiry; if the trader wants to act as a marketmaker in these instruments then they should show less size. On the other hand, with gammas this big, there is not another instrument in the marketplace offering such high gearing to the speculative directional trader as upbets and downbets.

Fig 5.3.2 illustrates downbet gammas for 5-day bets and volatility as indicated in the legend and should by now be reasonably self-explanatory.

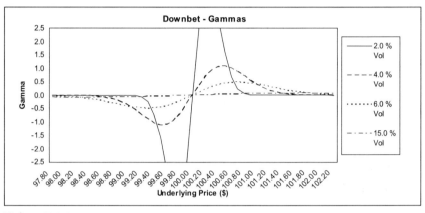

Figure 5.3.2

5.4   Bets v Conventionals

Fig 5.4.1 provides a comparison of upbet, downbet and conventional call and put gammas.

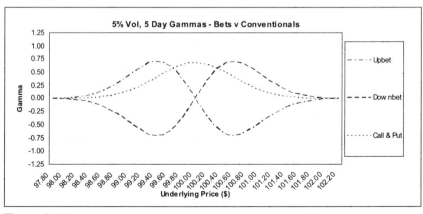

Figure 5.4.1

1. The downbet gamma is the negative of the upbet gamma.

2. The conventional call and put gammas are always positive irrespective

of time, underlying or volatility. Upbet and downbet gammas are both capable of taking positive or negative values dependent on the relationship between the underlying and the strike.

3. Conventional gammas and binary gammas have the commonality that they can all take the value of infinity conditional on the underlying. The conventional gamma can go to infinity when at-the-money whereas the at-the-money binary gamma is always zero but can approach infinity as the underlying approaches the strike.

5.5 Formulae

Upbet/Binary Call Gamma $\quad = \dfrac{-e^{-rt}d_1 N'(d_2)}{\sigma^2 S^2 t}$

Downbet/Binary Put Gamma $\quad = \dfrac{e^{-rt}d_1 N'(d_2)}{\sigma^2 S^2 t}$

where $\qquad d_1 = \dfrac{\log(\frac{S}{E}) + (r - D + \frac{1}{2}\sigma^2)t}{\sigma\sqrt{t}}$

$$d_2 = \frac{\log(\frac{S}{E}) + (r - D - \frac{1}{2}\sigma^2)t}{\sigma\sqrt{t}}$$

$$N'(x) = \frac{1}{\sqrt{2\pi}}\, e^{-0.5x^2}$$

and

S = price of the underlying

E = strike/exercise price

r = risk free rate of interest

D = continuous dividend yield of underlying

t = time in years to expiry

σ = annualised standard deviation of asset returns

5.6 Summary

Gamma is of fundamental importance to the binary options portfolio manager as it provides an 'at a glance' indicator of future deltas in the event of the underlying moving away from the current price. Long gamma positions mean that as the market falls the delta will become increasingly negative. Alternatively, the delta neutral long gamma trader will find his position becoming longer delta if the underlying rises. Alternatively, the short gamma position becomes long deltas when the underlying falls and short deltas when the underlying rises. Consequently the incidence of options traders getting 'blown out' is weighted far more heavily to short gamma traders than long gamma traders.

Out-of-the-money upbets and downbets are always positive gamma, while the in-the-money bets are always negative gamma. The gamma is always zero when the strike is at-the-money.

Finally, the proviso has to be added that as the time to expiry gets close the gammas like the other greeks becomes useless as a tangible measure. Yet again, the numbers thrown out by the equations are not erroneous but are only accurate for an infinitely small movement in the underlying, a movement in the underlying so small that the gamma loses worthwhile value.

5.7 Exercises

1. The strike price is $100 and the underlying is trading at $99.50. If the underlying moves up towards the strike, the gamma of the upbet will:

   a) Rise

   b) Fall

   c) Remain the same

   d) Don't know

2. The strike with the potentially highest absolute gamma is:

   a) the at-the-money strike

   b) the strike most out-of-the-money

   c) the strike nearest the underlying with one month to expiry

   d) the strike nearest the underlying with two months to expiry

3. The upbet delta and downbet gamma with the underlying are provided in the following table. What is the best approximation of the gamma at an underlying of $99.70, $99.90, $100.10 and $100.30?

	$99.60	$99.80	$100.00	$100.20	$100.40
Upbet Delta	0.2345	0.2395	0.2410	0.2390	0.2336
Downbet Gamma	0.0333	0.0163	−0.0012	−0.0186	−0.0351

4. The upbet at $99.40 has a gamma of 0.0489. What is the best guess of the delta at $99.40?

5.8 Answers

1. The gamma may well rise or fall as the underlying rises. It depends on the time to expiry and implied volatility. If there was very little time left to expiry, then the gamma would almost certainly remain constant and then rise as it approached the strike, and this answer would be true if volatility were also extremely low. On the other hand the peak of gamma could be at an underlying point below $99.50 if the time to expiry and/or implied volatility were high enough leading to a fall in gamma. The answer is therefore d).

2. At a) gamma is zero so wrong. At b) the strike most out of the money could also have a zero gamma, so wrong. Other things being equal, the strike with less time to expiry has more gamma than the strike with more time to expiry, so c) is the correct answer.

3. At $99.70

Gamma	=	(0.2395 − 0.2345) / ($99.80 − $99.60)
	=	0.025

At $99.90

Gamma	=	(0.2410 − 0.2395) / ($100.00 − $99.80)
	=	0.0075

At $100.10

Gamma	=	(0.2390 − 0.2410) / ($100.20 − $100.00)
	=	− 0.01

At $100.30

Gamma	=	(0.2336 – 0.2390) / ($100.40 – $100.20)
	=	– 0.027

4. The average gamma between $99.40 and $99.60 is:

Gamma	=	(0.0333 + 0.0489) / 2
	=	0.0411

Substituting in the above formula for gamma:

0.0411	=	(0.2345 – Delta) / ($99.60 – $99.40)
0.00822	=	.2345 – Delta
Delta	=	0.2345 – 0.00822
	=	0.22628

Section II:

This section covers rangebets and eachwaybets. Both sets of bets are combinations of upbets and downbets offered as a package or strategy. In terms of volumes, strategy trading dominates conventional options with most retail options traders having a knowledge of conventional strategies such as call and put spreads, straddles, strangles and butter-flies. Since a binary straddle (long or short both upbet and downbet with same strike and expiry) is always worth 100 and since in general a long X-strike upbet is identical to a short X-strike downbet the number of binary strategies is more limited. Nevertheless, 'eachway' betting in particular is rife across sports betting and it will no doubt be just as popular in financial and commodity betting.

Initially random walk graphs are used to define winning and losing bets, with the subsequent profit and loss profiles, followed by sensitivity analysis.

6

Rangebets

6.0   Introduction

The rangebet enables the trader to bet that the underlying will finish between two prices, the upper and the lower strikes, at some time in the future.

The rangebet enables the bettor to back a view that:

1. The Microsoft share price will close between $26.50 and $28.50 on the last day of September.

2. The price of WTI oil is between $125 and $135 at the year end.

3. The dollar/euro exchange rate closes between 1.55 and 1.60 on the last day of August.

4. The change in the next US non-farm payroll is between +100,000 and +125,000.

5. The Fed Funds rate is between 5.75% and 6.25% in six months time.

6.1   Price Specification

Random walks are again used to determine winners and losers and in this example (Fig 6.1.1) the bettor speculates whether the underlying will be between $99 and $101 at expiry.

1. RW1 oscillates around the upper strike until, with three days to expiry, the underlying moves upwards and closes out-of-the-money above the upper strike of $101. The rangebet therefore expires with the underlying outside the $99/$101 corridor and the bet is therefore a loser.

2. RW2 conversely drifts down to pass through the lower strike at $99, bounces, but then heads lower to once again pass through $99 with two days to expiry. This bet is also a loser as the underlying at the expiry of the bet is once again outside the corridor and out-of-the-money.

3. RW3 never moves out of the $99/$101 range and is therefore always 'in-the-money'. At expiry the underlying is roughly at $100.20, almost at the centre of the range, and the bet is a winner.

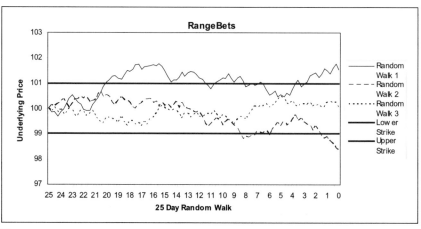

Figure 6.1.1

6.2   Rangebet Pricing

Fig 6.2.1 illustrates the expiry profile of the rangebet. The rangebet is a short position in the $99 downbet plus a short position in the $101 upbet. By convention the aggregate of the prices of the downbet and the upbet are subtracted from 100 to give the tradeable price of the rangebet which itself reflects the probability of the underlying being between the strikes at expiry.

N.B. As with the previous convention established in this book, when the underlying finishes exactly on either strike the bet is considered a 'draw' and settles at 50.

Example 6.2.1

If the underlying were to be at $100 then it would be equidistant from the $99 and $101 strikes. Assuming a symmetrical probability distribution, the $99 downbet will be the same price as the $101 upbet since the probability of the underlying going down $1 will be the same probability as it going up $1. So if it is assumed the $101 upbet is worth 23 then the $99 downbet will also be 23, pricing the $99/$101 rangebet at:

$$\text{Rangebet} = 100 - (\text{Downbet} + \text{Upbet})$$
$$= 100 - (23 + 23)$$
$$= 54.$$

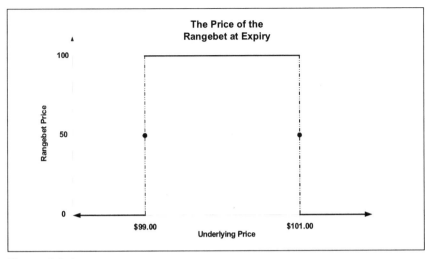

Figure 6.2.1

Alternatively the rangebet can be considered as the binary equivalent of a conventional 'guts' (I don't make up the names!) which is the inverse of the conventional strangle. A long guts consists of a long in-the-money call plus a long in-the-money put. A rangebet can therefore be considered as an in-the-money upbet plus an in-the-money downbet less 100 to achieve the tradeable price between 0 and 100.

Example 6.2.2

Using the prices of Example 6.2.1 the $99 upbet and $101 downbet must each be worth 77. The rangebet is therefore priced at:

$$\text{Rangebet} \quad = \quad \text{Upbet} + \text{Downbet} - 100$$
$$= \quad 77 + 77 - 100$$
$$= \quad 54.$$

6.3   Rangebet Profit & Loss Profiles

Figs 6.3.1 and 6.3.2 illustrate the P&Ls of respectively Trader A who has bought the $99/$101 rangebet for 35 at $10 per point and Trader B who has sold it.

Trader A has now 'upped his size' and is now betting $10/pt instead of the $1/pt he started with. He has bought the rangebet for 35 so his maximum loss is now 35 x $10 = $350. Likewise his maximum profit is now (100 – 35) × $10 = $650, with Trader A making a profit of $150 should the underlying be exactly on either strike at the rangebet's expiry.

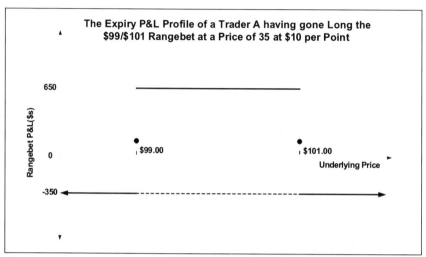

Figure 6.3.1

Fig 6.3.2 illustrates Trader B's P&L which is Trader A's P&L reflected through the horizontal axis. Trader B has bet that the underlying does not finish between the strikes at expiry. If it does then Trader B will lose $650. If the underlying goes out exactly on the strike then B loses $150. If Trader B is correct and the underlying 'goes out' either below $99 or above $101 then he wins $350.

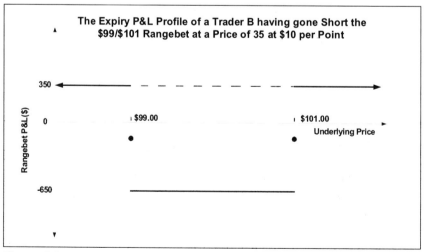

Figure 6.3.2

6.4   Rangebets v Conventional Strangles

Owing to a quirk of binary convention the rangebet is constructed from the sum of the downbet and the upbet subtracted from 100 compared to the conventional strangle which is simply the aggregate of the put and the call. The upshot is that when one purchases a strangle one is betting that the underlying will finish outside either of the two strikes, while conversely, when one purchases the strangle's binary cousin, the rangebet, one is betting that the underlying is between the two strikes.

Fig 6.4.1 compares a long $99.60/$100.40 strangle with a short rangebet with the same strike prices. The price of the strangle is 35 and the rangebet is priced at 65, both contract sizes are $1 per point.

Between the underlying of A and B the rangebet and strangle both lose $35. At A and B the strangle still loses $35 but the rangebet shows a $15 profit as the rangebet settles at 50 owing to the 'dead heat' rule. Below $99.60 and above $100.40 the rangebet seller receives the full premium of $65 profit as the rangebet is a losing bet. In comparison the strangle's P&L profile is -45° below A and +45° above B where it intersects the breakeven at C and D representing underlying levels of $99.25 and $100.75 respectively. At E and F the rangebet and strangle profiles intersect where they both yield a profit of $65. Outside E and F the strangle behaves like a short and a long future respectively and produces increasing profits whereas the rangebet's profit is now static at $65.

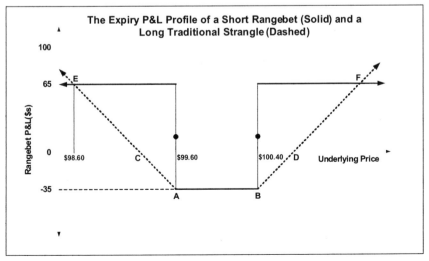

Figure 6.4.1

By inverting Fig 6.4.1 through the horizontal access at zero, one can envisage the long rangebet holder's P&L profile and the short strangles P&L profile. The writer of conventional options yet again faces the prospect of unlimited downside risk in comparison to the rangebet trader.

6.5   Rangebet Sensitivity Analysis

In general the greeks of the rangebet are an aggregate of the greeks of the respective upbet and downbet making up the rangebet. The calculation of rangebet greeks is subsequently not onerous. Nevertheless for any trader who trades in rangebets, or indeed has 'legged into' a rangebet having previously taken a position in either an upbet or downbet, an understanding of how rangebets are affected by time, volatility and the underlying is imperative.

6.6   Rangebet and Theta

Rangebet Theta = −1 × (Upbet Theta + Downbet Theta)

Fig 6.6.1 shows the route to expiry for the $99.50/$100.50 rangebet. With 50 days to expiry the profile is flat and within this range of underlying the rangebet is always worth about 20. As time passes the profiles tend towards the rectangular shape bounded by the rangebet prices of zero and 100 and the strike prices. When there is only half a day or less to expiry the profiles at both strikes pass through 50 since the effect of the other strike on the price has now become zero.

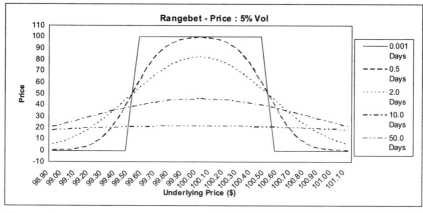

Figure 6.6.1

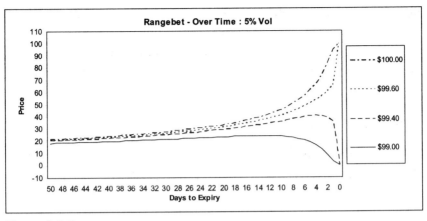

Figure 6.6.2

Fig 6.6.2 illustrates the $99.50/$100.50 strike rangebet price over time given the underlying in the legend. The levels of underlying have been chosen so that two are closely either side of the lower strike in order to illustrate the possibly unexpected price behaviour of the rangebet close to strikes, while the $99 profile is further out-of-the-money and the $100 profile exactly equidistant from the strikes.

If the days to expiry were extended outwards from the maximum 50 days to expiry the rangebet price would continue to fall away to the left of the graph and travel from 20 down to zero. With extreme time, say years, the probability of the underlying being between the strikes at expiry falls to almost nothing as the possibility of pinning the underlying to a particular range would resemble a game of Blind Man's Bluff.

The two profiles that are in-the-money uniformly rise in price until they both settle at 100. The interesting profile though is the $99.40, which is out-of-the-money but still rises in price until with three days to expiry it falls to zero. The $99.00 profile does the same but it is not so exaggerated.

The profiles for the $100.40, $100.60 and $101.00 profiles would be roughly the same as the $99.60, $99.40 and $99.00 profiles owing to the symmetry at about $100.

Fig 6.6.3 displays the rangebet theta for 5% volatility rangebets with days to expiry in the legend. The flat 50-day profile in Fig 6.6.1 betrays the presence of a low theta and as Fig 6.6.3 illustrates, it is flat at zero across the underlying range. The five-day theta has zero theta below and above the strikes at $99.33 and $100.67. With the passage of time the point of zero theta slides along the underlying towards the strikes of $99.50 and $100.50 from below and above the strikes.

Between the strikes although the theta is always positive it exhibits an unusual pattern. It rises at the midpoint of the strikes until the value of the rangebet approaches 100. At this stage, since the passage of time cannot increase the value of the rangebet beyond 100, the theta starts falling back towards zero which will be reached once the rangebet is valued at 100. Yet again the extreme thetas to be found just inside each of the rangebet strikes have been omitted as they yet again impact on the clarity of the graph as the value becomes inordinately high.

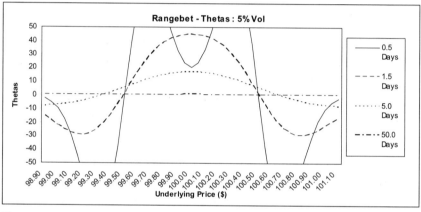

Figure 6.6.3

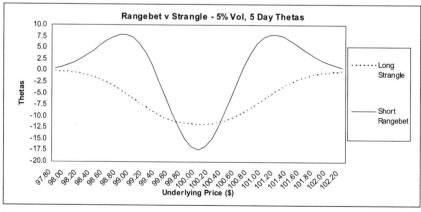

Figure 6.6.4

Finally, as with upbet and downbet theta, Fig 6.6.4 draws a comparison between conventional and binary greeks. In this instance a long position in a conventional strangle is compared with a short position in a rangebet.

Both have implied volatility of 5% and both have five days to expiry. Once again the volatile nature of binary greeks in comparison to conventional greeks is illustrated. The theta of strangles is either zero or negative whereas the theta of the rangebet can be positive, negative or zero dependent on the underlying.

6.7 Rangebets and Vega

$$\text{Rangebet Vega} = -1 \times (\text{Upbet Vega} + \text{Downbet Vega})$$

Fig 6.7.1 illustrates the effect of a change in 'vol' on the change in the rangebet price. The increasingly lower 'vol' acts on the rangebet price profile in a similar fashion to time decay. If the underlying is in-the-money and 'vol' falls there is less of a chance of the rangebet becoming out-of-the-money so the rangebet price increases. If the underlying is out-of-the-money a rise in 'vol' generally gives the rangebet a better chance of ending in-the-money thereby increasing the rangebet price. However, this assertion has to be tempered by the fact that increasing volatility increases the chance of the underlying travelling through both sets of strikes and settling out-of-the-money on the other side of the range.

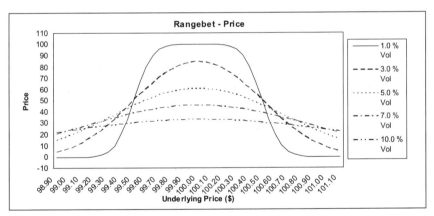

Figure 6.7.1

This point is illustrated in Fig 6.7.2, which plots for underlying prices as per the legend the $99.50/$100.50 rangebet prices against increasing volatility. For the two in-the-money prices of $100 and $99.60 the rangebet prices fall in the face of rising implied volatility since increased volatility increases the odds that the underlying will move outside the range. The $99.00 profile increases as volatility increases thereby giving the underlying a better chance of rising to the range but then drifts off as higher volatility increases the probability of the underlying moving further away from the range.

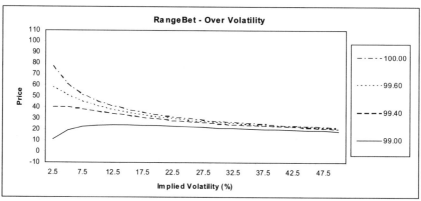

Figure 6.7.2

As volatility rises, thereby generating a wider potential underlying price range at expiry, the relative importance of the $99 and $100 prices to the strikes decreases in importance, so that at a volatility of 50% all four profiles converge around the rangebet price level of 20. They then continue to fall in tandem as volatility becomes increasingly high and the probability of hitting the range diminishes.

Finally Fig 6.7.3 provides rangebet vegas which are derived from the gradients in Fig. 6.7.2. Of note is that anywhere between the strikes the vega is always negative while outside the strikes the vega is positive or negative depending on the underlying and the level of volatility.

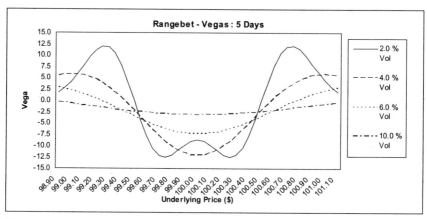

Figure 6.7.3

Between the strikes at 2% vol the vega reaches −12.5 but forms a hump midway between the strikes. This is because the rangebet has already reached a price of almost 100 and therefore cannot rise much further. When the rangebet price reaches 100 the vega will have returned to zero as a change in volatility has no effect on the rangebet price.

The long strangle vega and short rangebet vega are offered for comparison in Fig 6.7.4. The vega of the strangle is always positive while the rangebet vega can be positive or negative. Over the range of the underlying the strangle vega is always higher than than the rangebet vega, and at the extremes in the underlying they both approach zero. Clearly, for a vega fund one can therefore get greater exposure to volatility by trading conventional strangles as opposes to binaries, yet for the delta neutral marketmaker, the rangebet offers a far less risky product to make tight prices in than vega-heavy strangles. As the strikes get closer this situation is exacerbated because as the difference between the lower strike and upper strike tends to zero, the strangle becomes the highly sensitive straddle, while the binary equivalent (short same strike upbet and downbet) always has to sum to 100 and therefore has zero vega.

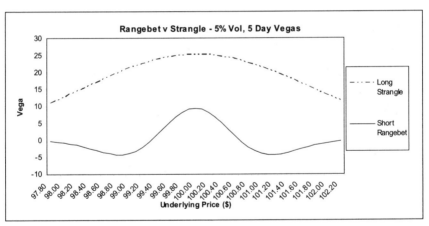

Figure 6.7.4

6.8   Rangebets and Delta

Rangebet Delta = −1 × (Upbet Delta + Downbet Delta)

The rangebet deltas are the negative of the aggregate of the downbet and upbet deltas that make up the rangebet. In Fig 6.8.1 the delta of the $99.50/$100.50 rangebet with 5% volatility is illustrated with various times to expiry. The deltas are positive around the level of the downbet and negative at the level of the upbet.

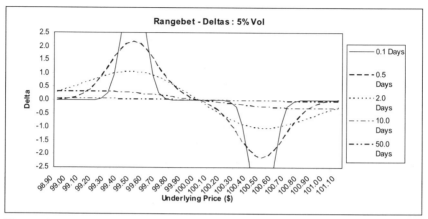

Figure 6.8.1

As time to expiry falls the delta is increasingly influenced by solely the individual upbet or downbet adjacent to the underlying, i.e. with the underlying trading around $99.45 say, the delta becomes the delta of the negative of the $99.50 downbet as time falls to 0.1 days. With 50 days to expiry the delta is close to zero across the breadth of the underlying range. Finally, irrespective of the time to expiry the delta is always zero midway between the two strikes.

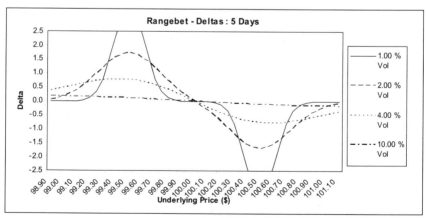

Figure 6.8.2

Fig 6.8.2 reveals deltas of approximately zero for high volatilities underscoring the fact that time and volatility most often have a similar impact on the value of bets. As with deltas over time, as volatility falls at $99.50

and $100.50 the deltas tend to ±∞ with the same steepling effect as for the individual upbet and downbet deltas and thereby creating the same hedging problems. Irrespective of volatility the delta passes through zero midway between the strikes.

6.9 Rangebets and Gamma

Rangebet Gamma = −1 × (Upbet Gamma + Downbet Gamma)

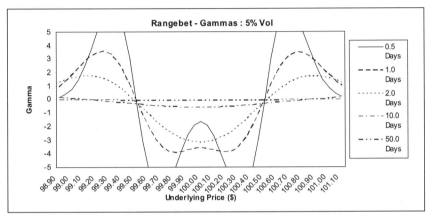

Figure 6.9.1

Fig 6.9.1 illustrates the gammas corresponding to the rangebet deltas of Fig 6.8.1.

1. The slope of the rangebet delta from the peak of the lower rangebet strike to the trough of the upper rangebet strike is negative or zero and this is illustrated in Fig 6.9.1 where the gamma between the strikes is always negative or zero.

2. Midway between the strikes the gamma becomes increasingly negative over time until between 1 and 0.5 day to expiry the gammas starts rising back up to zero as the delta flattens out. At this point there is little chance of the rangebet now losing and with the rangebet maintaining a value of 100 even with the underlying moving up and down within the strikes, the gamma becomes zero.

Fig 6.9.2 displays the rangebet gammas which are the gradients of the deltas in Fig 6.8.2.

The 1% vol profile illustrates how, with falling volatility, the gamma increasingly is polarised between 0 and ±∞.

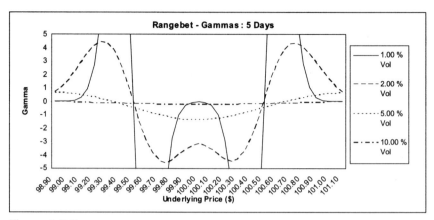

Figure 6.9.2

At high volatility the gamma approaches zero across the range of underlying.

6.10 Summary

Although rangebets are hardly in the category of 'exotics' they are certainly more esoteric than the vanilla upbets and downbets previously discussed.

1. Rangebets may be particularly attractive to a trader who believes that the underlying is going to be fairly static around some future price. It may be around the current price where the summer season may be imminent with a general slowing down of trader activity, or it may be that the trader takes a specific view on a forthcoming economic data, e.g. non-farm payrolls, and wishes to tailor a bet to take advantage of an exact view on the range of the number.

2. Rangebets are reasonably simple to evaluate involving the downbet being added to the upbet and the total being subtracted from 100.

3. The rangebet has a corollary in the conventional market in the shape of a strangle although when trading the former the buyer wins if the underlying lies between the strikes at expiry, whereas with the strangle the seller wins if the underlying remains between the strikes.

4. The greeks are all calculated by adding the upbet greek to the downbet greek and multiplying the total by −1.

6.11 Exercises

1. A bettor backs the $109 / $111 rangebet at prices of 60 and 10 for $100 per point respectively. Fill in the table with the trader's P&L for each underlying.

	<$109	$109	$109–$111	$111	>$111
60					
10					

2. The $99 downbet is trading at 24 bid, offered at 26 while the $101 upbet is 21 bid, offered at 23. What do these prices imply the $99/$101 rangebet to be?

3. If in Question 2 the downbet is 24 bid for $250 per point, $500 per point offered at 26 while the size of the upbet bid and offer is $1,000 per point, what could the broker safely make in the rangebet price and size if there were no rangebet quote and he didn't want to get 'hung' on a leg?

4. The $101 upbet is worth 25, the $99/$101 rangebet is worth 60. What is the $99 downbet worth?

5. The underlying is trading $100. A trader fancies a move and wants to get long gammas. The $98/$102 rangebet is offered at 54 and the trader buys it. Is this a good trade?

6. The underlying moves to the upper strike of a rangebet. A trader buys the rangebet. If the trader wants to get delta neutral should he sell or buy the underlying?

7. The greatest amount of time value to be received for the premium seller is midway between the strikes. True or False?

6.12 Answers

1.

	<$109	$109	$109 – $111	$111	>$111
60	−$6,000	−$1,000	+$4,000	−$1,000	−$6,000
10	−$1,000	+$4,000	+$9,000	+$4,000	−$1,000

2. The outright bids combine to form the rangebet offer and vice versa. Therefore, the rangebet is offered at:

$$100 - (24 + 21) = 55$$

and is bid:

$$100 - (26 + 23) = 51$$

3. The downbet is bid for $250 and upbet for $1,000, therefore the broker can offer his client $250 at 55.

   The downbet is offered for $500 and upbet for $1,000, so the broker can show his client a bid of 51 for $500 rangebets.

4. The outrights must be worth 100 – 60 = 40.

   The upbet is worth 25 therefore the downbet must be worth:

$$Downbet = 40 - 25 = 15$$

5. No, it is a lousy trade. The rangebet is trading at its highest point with the underlying bang in the middle of the strikes. A move will subsequently mean the rangebet is worth less. But most importantly the trader wants to 'get long gammas'. Buying in-the-money rangebets gets the trader short gammas.

6. If the underlying continues to move higher, then the rangebet will be worth less. If the underlying moves down as far as the midpoint between the strikes the rangebet will increase in value. The delta at the upper strike is therefore negative. Should the trader wish to get delta neutral he needs to buy the underlying.

7. False. The theta is at its highest midway between the strikes for much of the rangebet's life. But as expiry draws near the highest theta starts to move away from the midpoint of the rangebet to just inside the two strikes.

7

EachWayBets

7.0 Introduction

An eachwaybet is a tiered bet offering a middle range where the bet settles at 50. Examples of eachwaybets would include:

A bet that gold will finish above $1,100 at the year end. If it does, then the bet settles at 100. If not, but gold is above $1,000 year end then the bet settles at 50, otherwise zero.

A bet that oil settles below $130 at the end of October. If it doesn't but is in the range $130-$140 then it is still settled at 50, above $140 it settles at zero.

A bet that the annualised Consumer Price Index number for June is above 4.5%. If not, but the CPI is above 4.00% then the bet settles at 50, but if the CPI is below 4.00% the bet settles at zero.

7.1 Price Specificaton

Eachwaybets provide the opportunity to back a view on whether the underlying will finish above a higher strike, between the higher and a lower strike or below the lower strike. In our random walk examples the higher and lower strikes are $101 and $99 respectively. Fig 7.1.1 provides random walk graphs to illustrate the outcome of bets.

1. RW1 never trades outside the $99/$101 corridor and at the expiry of the bet the underlying is almost midway between the two strikes. This eachwaybet subsequently settles at 50.

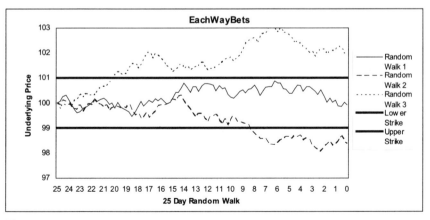

Figure 7.1.1

2. RW2 drifts along between the strikes until with eight days remaining it moves lower and passes through the $99 strike. The underlying does

not recover and is below the lower strike at the bet's expiry determining that the bet is a loser and settles at zero.

3. RW3 breaks through the upper strike after five days. The underlying remains above the $101 level through to the expiry of this eachwaybet resulting in the bet winning and a settlement price of 100.

7.2 Eachwaybet Pricing

Fig 7.2.1 illustrates the expiry profile of the eachwaybet. The eachwaybet is a short position in the $99 downbet plus a long position in the $101 upbet. Just leaving the pricing in this manner would mean that the price of the eachwaybet would range between –100 to +100. This does not fit in with the binary concept of the price remaining between zero and 100, and anyway a negative price would imply a negative probability which is an impossibility. Therefore to achieve the range of prices as defined by Fig 7.2.1 it is necessary to add 100 and divide the total by 2.

Yet again, if we assume the underlying to be $100 then the equidistant rule will imply the price of the $99 downbet and $101 upbet are the same, e.g. both 18. The price of the eachwaybet with the underlying at $100 and downbet and upbet both worth 18 will then be:

$$
\begin{aligned}
\text{Eachwaybet} \quad &= \quad (\text{UpBet} - \text{DownBet} + 100) / 2 \\
&= \quad (18 - 18 + 100) / 2 \\
&= \quad 50
\end{aligned}
$$

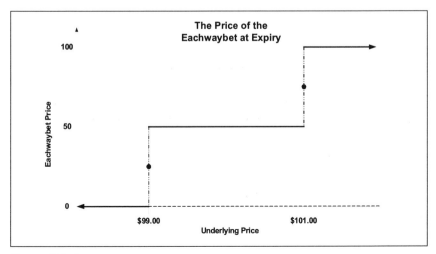

Figure 7.2.1

which is exactly where you would expect the price of an eachwaybet to always be when the underlying is exactly between the strikes since the price is implying that there is exactly the same probability of the underlying ending above $101 as below $99.

If the underlying is anywhere between the upper and lower strike at expiry then the eachwaybet will settle at 50. If the underlying is exactly on the lower strike then the eachwaybet will settle at 25 and if exactly on the upper strike then 75 as per the 'dead heat' rule.

7.3   Eachwaybet Profit & Loss Profiles

Figs 7.3.1 and 7.3.2 illustrate the P&Ls of Traders A & B who have bought and sold the $99/$101 eachwaybet to each other at 30 for $10 per point. Fig 7.3.1 illustrates:

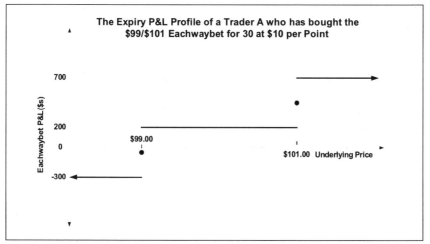

Figure 7.3.1

Trader A's P&L with the premium of $300 being lost if the underlying is below $99 at expiry, a $200 profit above $99 but below $101, and a $700 profit if the underlying finishes above $101. In many respects this bet has similarities with an 'each way' bet on a horse. A $300 bet would win $700 if the horse wins implying a price of 7/3. If the horse comes second then the $300 only wins $200 for 'the place' reflecting a price of 6/4 On.

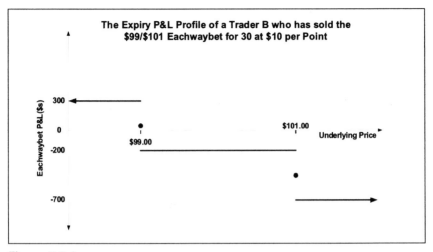

Figure 7.3.2

The eachwaybet offers five separate settlement prices with the 'dead heat' settlements. This spreads the risk more than a straight upbet and is more likely to be attractive to the less professional gambler.

7.4 Eachwaybets and Conventional Combos

In conventional parlance the strategy of being short a put (lower strike) and long a call (higher strike) is known as a combo, cylinder or minimax depending on the particular options market. A short position in the put and long position in the call both generate positive deltas, therefore being long a combo is a bullish strategy.

Fig 7.4.1 compares a long $99.60/$100.40 combo with a long $99.60/$100.40 eachwaybet. The prices of the put and the downbet are both 15 with the call and the upbet both 50. This leads to prices of 35 and 67.5 for the combo and eachwaybet respectively, while the contract size for the combo is $1 per point and the eachwaybet $2 per point. Between the underlying of A and B the eachwaybet and combo both lose $35 because at expiry the combo is worth zero while the eachwaybet is worth 50. The combo subsequently loses:

$$\text{Combo P\&L} = (0 - 35) \times \$1$$
$$= -\$35$$

while the eachwaybet loses:

$$\text{Eachwaybet P\&L} \quad = \quad (50 - 67.5) \times \$2$$
$$= \quad -\$35.$$

At A and B the combo still loses $35 but at A and B the 'dead heat' rule applies so that at A the eachwaybet settles at 25 showing a $85 loss while at B where the bet settles at 75 the profit is $15.

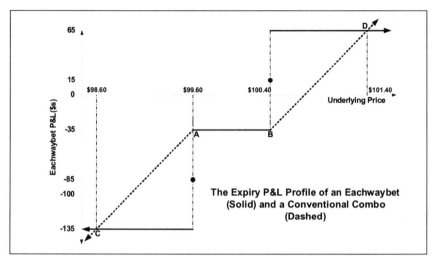

Figure 7.4.1

Anywhere below A the eachwaybet loses $135 while the combo behaves like a long future and does not lose $135 until the underlying has fallen to $98.60 where the P&Ls intersect. Further falls in the underlying from C create a continuing loss while the eachwaybet is stopped out at $135. On the upside above $100.40 the eachwaybet's profit is capped at $65 whereas the combo can make an unlimited profit.

7.5   Eachway Upbets and Eachway Downbets

In the same manner that a long upbet position is the equivalent of a short downbet position assuming the same strike and expiry, the same is true of the eachwaybet.

If Fig 7.4.1 was assumed to be an eachway upbet then the seller at 67.5 would have a P&L profile as in Fig 7.5.1. This is obviously the same as a purchase of an $99.50/$100.50 eachway downbet for 32.5 so further separate analysis of eachway upbets and eachway downbets will be dispensed with.

There is an additional prerequisite for the short eachway upbet to equate to a long eachway downbet and that is that the settlement value of the bet between the strikes is 50.

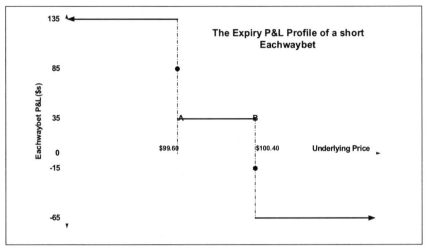

Figure 7.5.1

Later a section on the 25:10:0 spreadbet introduces eachwaybets with settlement prices between the strikes other than 50, which means the long eachway upbet does not replicate a short eachwaydownbet.

7.6   Eachwaybet Sensitivity Analysis

The greeks of eachwaybets are constructed quite simply so in the following sections a brief note on the equation plus graphs of the greeks illustrating the eachwaybet's behaviour will be proffered. The reader, it is hoped, will by now have sufficient background to follow the illustrations and work out why the price of the eachwaybet behaves in a particular manner to changes in time, volatility and the underlying.

7.7   Eachwaybet and Theta

Eachwaybet Theta   =   (Upbet Theta – Downbet Theta) / 2

Fig 7.7.1 shows the route to expiry for the $99.50/$100.50 5% volatility eachwaybet. Midway between the strikes all profiles travel through the price of 50 irrespective of time to expiry. It is not until with just half a day to go that the profiles start to assume the profile at expiry.

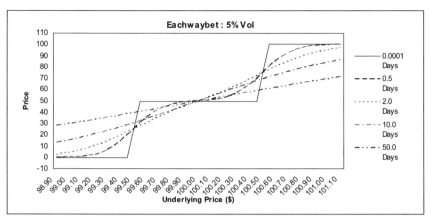

Figure 7.7.1

Figure 7.7.2 illustrates the eachwaybet prices over time of five underlying prices. The three middle profiles all lay between the strikes and ultimately are worth 50 while profiles at $100.60 and $99.40 result in bet prices at expiry of 100 and zero respectively.

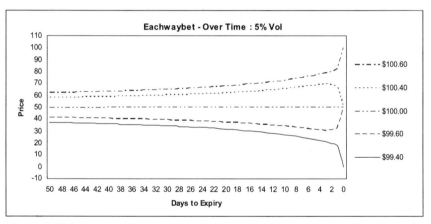

Figure 7.7.2

Fig 7.7.3 displays the 5% vol eachwaybet thetas with days to expiry in the legend. The 5-day theta plots the gradients of the profiles in Fig 7.7.2 with five days to expiry.

The theta of the 50-day profile is very low across the underlying range, while with two days to expiry the theta has a peak and trough at the lower and upper strike respectively.

Finally, a comparison is drawn between conventional and binary greeks. Both the combo and eachwaybet in Fig 7.7.4 have 5% implied volatility and five days to expiry. The theta of the eachwaybet is almost a reflection of the combo theta, with both profiles passing through zero where the underlying is exactly midway between the strikes.

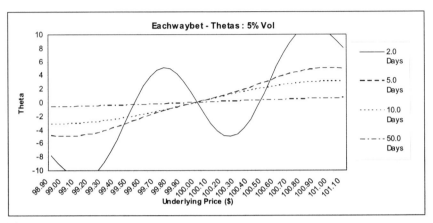

Figure 7.7.3

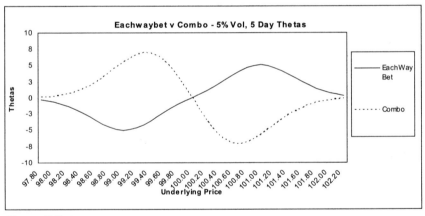

Figure 7.7.4

7.8 Eachwaybet and Vega

Eachwaybet Vega   =   (Upbet Vega – Downbet Vega) / 2

Fig 7.8.1 displays the price profiles for $99.50/$100.50 5-day each-waybets. Fig 7.8.2 illustrates the behaviour of eachwaybet prices as implied volatility rises.

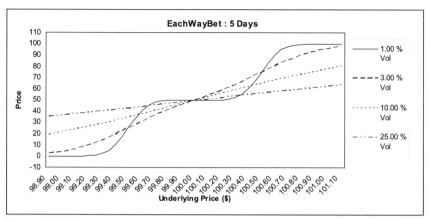

Figure 7.8.1

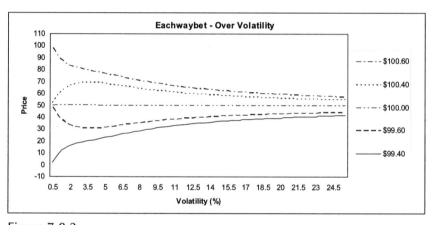

Figure 7.8.2

Fig 7.8.3 illustrates 5-day eachwaybet vegas.

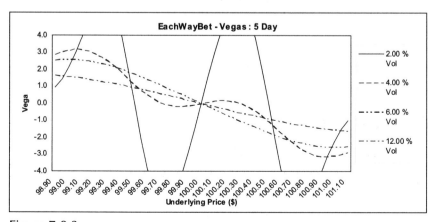

Figure 7.8.3

Fig 7.8.4 shows vegas of the conventional and eachwaybet reflected through the horizontal axis again. Yet again both profiles pass through zero when the underlying is midway between the strikes.

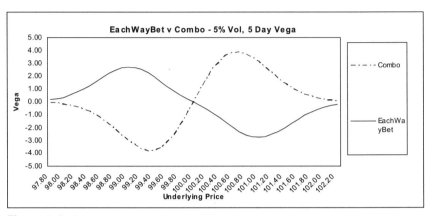

Figure 7.8.4

7.9 Eachwaybets and Delta

Eachwaybet Delta   =   (Upbet Delta – Downbet Delta) / 2

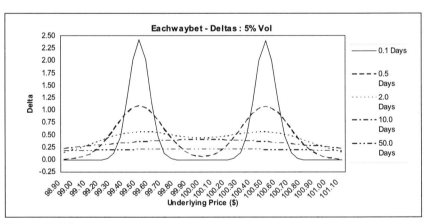

Figure 7.9.1

The eachwaybet delta is always positive as illustrated in Fig 7.9.1. At both lower and upper strikes the delta peaks, and as time passes the delta at each strike takes the characteristics of the short downbet and long upbet constituting the eachwaybet.

As time to expiry increases the delta is zero irrespective of where the underlying is.

120

Fig 7.9.2 provides deltas for different volatilities. As volatility falls from 9% to 1% the effect on the delta is very similar to time decay.

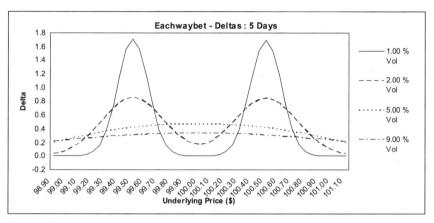

Figure 7.9.2

7.10 Eachwaybets and Gamma

Eachwaybet Gamma   =   (Upbet Gamma – Downbet Gamma) / 2

Fig 7.10.1 illustrates the gammas corresponding to the deltas of Fig 7.9.1., albeit the 0.1 days omitted as the numbers are too high and destroy the graph's clarity.

Midway between the strikes the gamma is always zero irrespective of time to expiry.

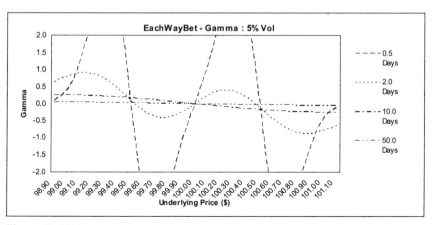

Figure 7.10.1

Fig 7.10.2 provides gammas for the deltas in Fig 7.9.2.

The 9% and 1% gammas provide further evidence of the Jekyll and Hyde nature of binaries with the contrasting profiles they generate. The 5% gamma is relatively flat and enables the trader to forecast deltas with ease. The 2% gamma oscillates from positive to negative and makes delta hedging of a book a near impossibility when volatility falls so low.

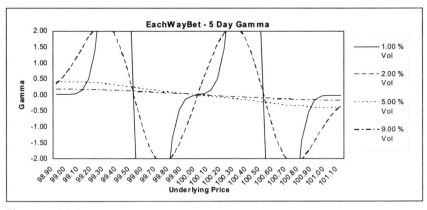

Figure 7.10.2

7.11   25:10:0 Spreadbets

Spreadbetting companies often offer the 25:10:0 spreadbet whereby if a horse wins an event then it settles at 25, but should it come in second or third it settles at 10, with a settlement price of zero if it comes outside the first three. By multiplying the payoffs by four the 25:10:0 spreadbet could just as easily be referred to as the 100:40:0 spreadbet leading to the 25:10:0 spreadbet turning into an eachwaybet with 40 as the settlement price between the strikes instead of 50.

25:10:0 Pricing

25:10:0 Upbet = [80 + (1.2 × Upbet − 0.8 × Downbet)] / 2

25:10:0 Downbet = [80 + (1.2 × Downbet − 0.8 × Upbet)] / 2

The formulae for the 25:10:0 upbet and downbet can be compared to the eachwaybet in Section 7.2. The 25:10:0 bet is clearly a short downbet and long upbet with a slightly different transposition.

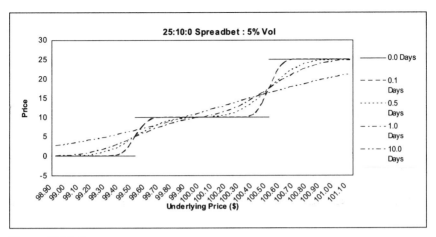

Figure 7.11.1

25:10:0 Deltas

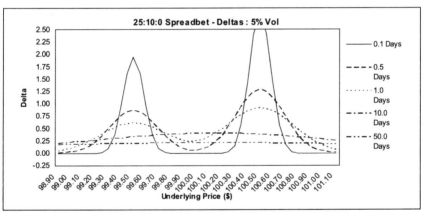

Figure 7.11.2

25:10:0 Upbet Delta = (1.2 × Upbet Delta − 0.8 × Downbet Delta) / 2

25:10:0 Downbet Delta = (1.2 × Downbet Delta − 0.8 Upbet Delta) / 2

25:10:0 Gammas

25:10:0 Upbet Gamma = (1.2 × Upbet Gamma − 0.8 × Downbet Gamma) / 2

25:10:0 Downbet Gamma = (1.2 × Downbet Gamma − 0.8 × Upbet Gamma) / 2

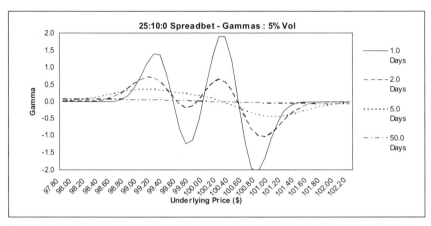

Figure 7.11.3

25:10:0 Theta

25:10:0 Upbet Theta = (1.2 × Upbet Theta – 0.8 × Downbet Theta) / 2

25:10:0 Downbet Theta = (1.2 × Downbet Theta – 0.8 × Upbet Theta) / 2

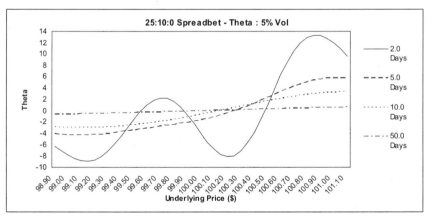

Figure 7.11.4

25:10:0 Vega

25:10:0 Upbet Vega = (1.2 × Upbet Vega – 0.8 × Downbet Vega) / 2

25:10:0 Downbet Vega = (1.2 × Downbet Vega – 0.8 × Upbet Vega) / 2

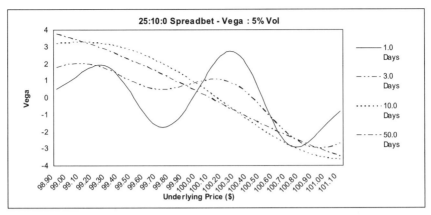

Figure 7.11.5

7.12 Summary

Eachwaybets are reasonably easy to evaluate being a combination of a short downbet and long upbet.

Eachwaybets provide the punter with an alternative to the all-or-nothing upbet and downbet. Eachwaybets can still provide the bettor with a winning position even if he hasn't called the market 100% correctly.

The marketmaker incurs far less risk in pricing eachwaybets since as expiry draws near the bet can only change in value by a maximum of 25 when on a strike. This feature means that greeks are generally more forgiving than the greeks of straight upbets and downbets.

Eachwaybets have a relation in the conventional market in the form of the combo (cylinder spread, mini-max etc).

The greeks are all calculated by subtracting the downbet greek from the upbet greek and dividing the total by 2.

Spreadbetting companies offer a 25:10:0 which has been shown to be the eachwaybet with a settlement price of 40 (as opposed to 50) between the strikes.

7.13 Exercises

1. A bettor backs the $109 / $111 eachwaybet at prices of 60 and 10 for $100 per point respectively. Fill in the table with the trader's P&L for each underlying.

	Underlying Price				
	<$109	$109	$109–$111	$111	>$111
60					
10					

2. The $99 downbet is trading at 24 bid, offered at 26 while the $101 upbet is 21 bid, offered at 23. What do these prices imply the $99/$101 eachwaybet to be?

3. A $99.00 downbet has a market: 20 for $500/pt, $1,000/pt at 22. The $100.00 upbet market is: 28 for $400/pt, $500/pt at 30. What market can a broker safely quote a client without getting 'hung'?

4. What can the broker quote a client who wants price and size in the 25:10:0 eachway upbet?

5. The underlying is trading at $100.00. The trader wants to get long and has two choices, buying the $100/$101 strikes eachway upbet (settles at 40 between the strikes) or selling the $101/$100 strikes eachway downbet (settles at 40 between the strikes). If the underlying moves higher which strategy is likely to initially make more money?

7.14 Answers

1.

	<$109	109	$109–$111	111	>$111
60	−$6,000	−$3,500	−$1,000	+$1,500	+$4,000
10	−$1,000	+$1,500	+$4,000	+$6,500	+$9,000

2. Eachwaybet offer = (23 − 24 +100) / 2 = 49.5

   Eachwaybet bid = (21 − 26 + 100) / 2 = 47.5

3. The offer is (30-20+100)/2 = 55

   The bid is (22-28+100)/2 = 53

   The size the broker can offer is not immediately obvious. If the broker lifts all the $500 on offer at 30 in the upbet and sells the $500 being bid on the downbet then how many eachwaybets is that equivalent to? If the underlying rises so the upbet is now worth 31 and the downbet 19 then on legs the broker has a profit of:

$$(31\text{-}30) \times \$500 + (19\text{-}20) \times \text{-}\$500 = \$1,000$$

The price of the eachwaybet is now:

$$\text{Eachwaybet} = (31\text{-}19\text{+}100)/2 = 56$$

meaning that a rise from 55 to 56 has created $1,000 profit on two trades of $500 each. The broker can therefore show the client an offer of $1,000/pt at 55. The broker can show the client a bid of 53 for $800/pt. which is twice the size of the lower of the upbet bid and the downbet offer.

4. Eachway Upbet offer $\quad = [80 + (1.2 \times 30 - 0.8 \times 20)]/2$

$\qquad\qquad\qquad\qquad\quad = 50$

Eachway Upbet bid $\qquad = [80 + (1.2 \times 28 - 0.8 \times 22)]/2$

$\qquad\qquad\qquad\qquad\quad = 48$

If the broker buys the $500/pt offered at 30 on the upbet and sells the $500/pt bid at 20 on the downbet, should the upbet rise to 31 and the downbet fall to 19 the trades make $1,000 profit.

The eachway upbet is now worth:

$$[80 + (1.2 \times 31 - 0.8 \times 19)]/2 = 51$$

Therefore the broker can show the 25:10:0 eachway upbet in the same amount of size as if the bet was priced as a straight eachwaybet, i.e. as in 3. above.

5. The strategy with the greatest exposure to a movement in the underlying will be the most profitable. This means that the trader needs to choose the strategy with the higher delta. From Fig. 7.11.2 the eachway upbet has the highest delta at the upper strike. Conversely the eachway downbet will have the highest delta at the lower strike. In this case the underlying is trading at the lower strike so selling the eachway downbet will generate the greater initial profit.

8

Eachway Rangebets

8.0 Introduction

The eachway rangebet is an extension of the rangebet with two extra strikes and another level of settlement price. If the underlying finishes between the centre two strikes at the bet's expiry then the bet's settlement price is 100. If the underlying finishes outside the centre two strikes but inside the outer strikes then the bet settles at, say 40. If the underlying is outside the outer strikes the bet settles at zero.

8.1 Price Specification

Random walks are again used to determine winners and losers and in Fig 8.1.1 the bettor speculates whether the underlying will be within the $98.5/$101.5 rangebet or the $99.5/$100.5 rangebet at expiry. The settlement prices are 100:40:0.

1. RW1 oscillates either side of the $99.50 strike and settles at expiry at $99.00. RW1 is outside the inner range but inside the outer range and therefore settles at 40.

2. RW2 passes through $101.50 with seven days to expiry and trades around this level until with four days remaining it falls to expire almost exactly in the middle of the inner range. A winner settling at 100.

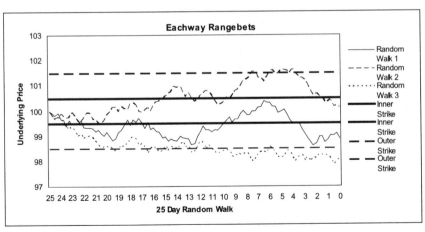

Figure 8.1.1

3. RW3 falls to the lowest strike after five days. It then oscillates around this level before settling at $98 outside the outer range and resulting in a bet settlement price of zero.

8.2 Eachway Rangebet Pricing

Fig 8.2.1 illustrates the expiry profile of the eachway rangebet. For the 100:40:0 eachway rangebet then the inner rangebet is calculated by adding the inner downbet to the inner upbet, multiplying by 1.2 and subtracted from 100 while the outer rangebet is the aggregation of the outer downbet and upbet, multiplied by 0.80 and subtracted from 100. Then the inner and outer rangebets are aggregated and divided by two to provide the price of the eachway rangebet. The 100:50:0 eachway rangebet consists of the inner rangebet price added to the outer rangebet price and divided by two.

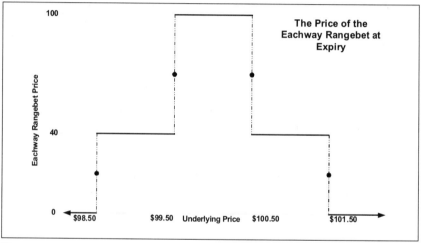

Figure 8.2.1

N.B. As with the previous convention established in this book when the underlying finishes exactly on a strike the bet is considered a 'dead heat' which in the case of the 100:40:0 bet means 'dead heat' prices of 20 and 70.

Example 8.2.1

If the underlying were to be at $100 then it would be equidistant from the $98.50 and $101.50 strikes plus the $99.50 and $100.50 strikes. Yet again assuming a symmetrical probability distribution, the $98.50 and $99.50 downbets and $100.50 and $101.50 upbets with 5% vol and ten days to expiry will be 3.5, 27.0, 27.0 and 3.5 respectively giving an eachway rangebet price of:

Eachway Rangebet	=	(Inner Rangebet + Outer Rangebet) / 2
where Inner Rangebet	=	100 – 1.2 × (27.0 + 27.0)
	=	100 – 64.8
	=	35.2
and Outer Rangebet	=	100 – 0.8 × (3.5 + 3.5)
	=	100 – 5.6
	=	94.4
Eachway Rangebet	=	(35.2 + 94.4) / 2
	=	64.8

8.3   Eachway Rangebet Profit & Loss Profiles

The underlying is trading around the $99.50 level and the $98.50/ $99.50/$100.50 /$101.50 eachway rangebet has twenty-five days to expiry. Figs 8.3.1 and 8.3.2 provide Trader A and Trader B's P&Ls after B has sold this bet to A for 45 at $10 per point. At the inception of the bet the underlying is on the lower of the inner two strikes so A only requires the underlying to rise one tick for the bet to win the maximum $100. Yet if the bet falls by less than 100 ticks then A only loses $50. Trader A therefore firstly wants a small move upwards but secondly does not want a move greater than 100 ticks.

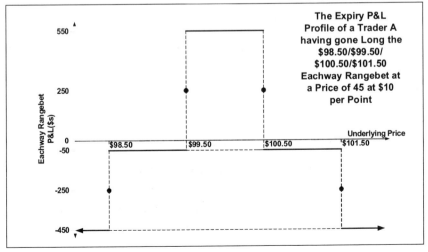

Figure 8.3.1

Fig 8.3.2 illustrates Trader B's P&L which is Trader A's P&L reflected through the horizontal axis. Trader B is really looking for a move of over 100 ticks on the downside where Trader B will win $450.

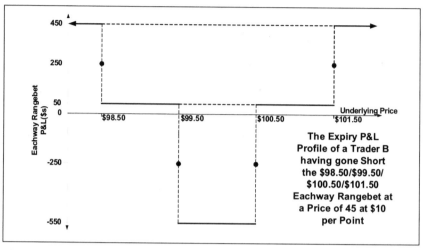

Figure 8.3.2

8.4   Eachway Rangebet Sensitivity Analysis

The greeks of the eachway rangebet are comprised of the inner and outer rangebets's greeks with a slight tweak to take into account the settlement price of 40. The graphical shapes of the eachway rangebet greeks can be quite flamboyant and the reader is invited to figure out for themselves why these greeks take the forms they do. In particular the five-day theta requires a fair dose of lateral thinking to figure out the profiles. The more the reader studies these illustrations and understands for themselves why the greeks are shaped the way they are, the more intuitive the following chapters on trading and hedging will be.

8.5   Eachway Rangebet and Theta

Eachway Rangebet Theta = −1 × ((Inner Upbet Theta + Inner Downbet Theta) × 1.2 + (Outer Upbet Theta + Outer Downbet Theta) × 0.8) / 2

Fig 8.5.1 shows the route to expiry for the $99.25/$99.75/$100.25/$100.75 eachway rangebet. The almost flat 50 days to expiry profile remains within the range 15.95 to 19.05 over the 210 tick range of the underlying and reflects a very low theta.

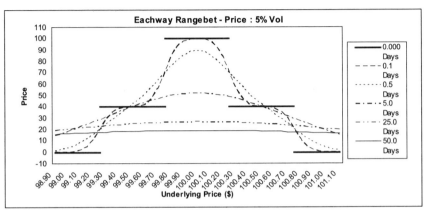

Figure 8.5.1

Only over the last half day does the price profile start to resemble the stepped shape of the expiry profile.

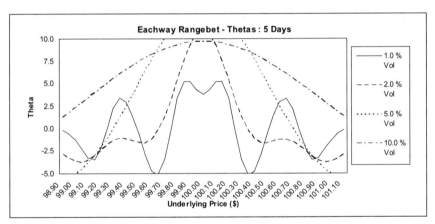

Figure 8.5.2

Fig 8.5.2 displays the eachway rangebet theta for five days to expiry and volatility as stated in the legend.

135

8.6 Eachway Rangebets and Vega

Eachway Rangebet Vega   =   −1 × ((Inner Upbet Vega + Inner Downbet Vega) × 1.2
+ (Outer Upbet Vega + Outer Downbet Vega) × 0.8) / 2

As volatility falls the effect on the bet price is detrimental if the underlying is outside the outer range but has the effect of increasing the value of the bet if the underlying lies between the strikes as illustrated by Fig 8.6.1.

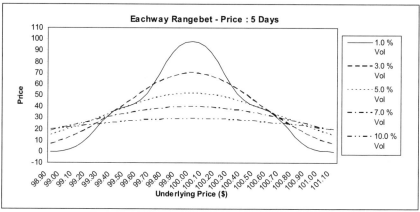

Figure 8.6.1

Figs 8.6.2 and 8.6.3 provide eachway rangebet vegas with those of the former almost being the inverse of the price profiles of Fig 8.6.1.

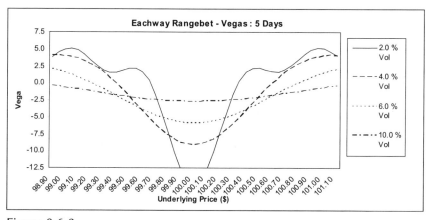

Figure 8.6.2

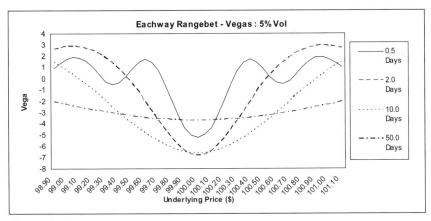

Figure 8.6.3

Vega clearly bottoms out in Fig 8.6.3. Furthermore the vega becomes a great deal shallower as the days to expiry are increased.

8.7   Eachway Rangebets and Delta

Eachway Rangebet Delta   =   −1 × ((Inner Upbet Delta + Inner
                               Downbet Delta) × 1.2
                               + (Outer Upbet Delta + Outer
                               Downbet Delta) × 0.8) / 2

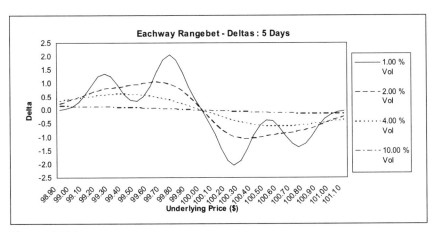

Figure 8.7.1

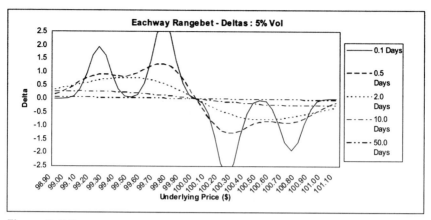

Figure 8.7.2

8.8   Eachway Rangebets and Gamma

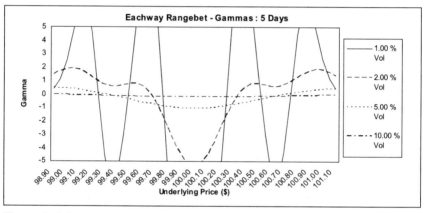

Figure 8.8.1

Eachway Rangebet Gamma   =   −1 × ((Inner Upbet Gamma + Inner Downbet Gamma) × 1.2
+ (Outer Upbet Gamma + Outer Downbet Gamma) × 0.8) / 2

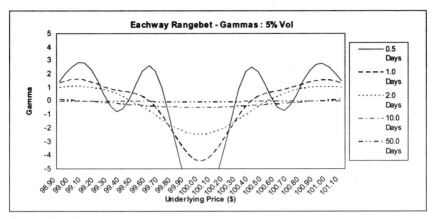

Figure 8.8.2

8.9 Summary

1. Like the eachway upbet and downbet, the eachway rangebet provides the less aggressive trader with a comfort zone.

2. Eachway rangebets can be used to take a punt on the future volatility of the underlying or alternatively may be a less-risk instrument for taking a directional view on the underlying.

3. In all of the above examples a settlement price of 40 has been assumed for the outer band but any settlement price is a possibility with 50 obviously another candidate.

4. The greeks are generally less-aggressive than the outright rangebet therefore there should be a keener price from the marketmaker as there is less risk for the marketmaker.

8.10 Exercises

1. A bettor backs the 100:40:0 $99.25/$99.50/$100.50/$100.75 each-way rangebet at prices of 60 and 10 for $100 per point respectively. Fill in the table with the traders P&L for each underlying.

	<99.25	99.26	99.5	100.49	100.75
60					
10					

2. The 'fair value' of the $98.50 and $99.00 downbets are 4.24 and 19.55 respectively while the $99.50 and $100.00 upbets are worth 49.88 and 19.50 respectively. What is the 'fair value' of the 100:40:0 and 100:50:0 $98.50/$99.00/$99.50/$100.00 eachway rangebets?

3. At what price is the underlying in Question 2?

4. A trader buys the marketmaker's offer for the 100:40:0 eachway rangebet of Question 2. Has the trader gone long or short deltas?

5. In Question 4 will the marketmaker need to buy or sell the underlying to eliminate exposure to a movement in the underlying?

6. The underlying moves down to $99.25 and the trader believes this to be a trigger for the market to become volatile. Should the trader buy or sell the eachway rangebet?

7. The underlying moves back up to $99.45, just inside the upper inner strike. A new trader buys the eachway rangebet to take in time value. Is this a good trade and what is the risk?

8.11   Answers

1.

	<99.25	99.26	99.5	100.49	100.75
60	-$6,000	-$2,000	$1,000	$4,000	-$4,000
10	-$1,000	$3,000	$6,000	$9,000	$1,000

2. 100:40:0

Eachway Rangebet	=	(Inner Rangebet + Outer Rangebet) / 2
where Inner Rangebet	=	$100 - 1.2 \times (19.55 + 49.88)$
	=	$100 - 83.316$
	=	16.684
and Outer Rangebet	=	$100 - 0.8 \times (4.24 + 19.5)$
	=	$100 - 18.992$
	=	81.008
Eachway Rangebet	=	$(16.684 + 81.008) / 2$
	=	<u>48.846</u>

100:50:0

Eachway Rangebet	=	(Inner Rangebet + Outer Rangebet) / 2
where Inner Rangebet	=	$100 - 1.0 \times (19.55 + 49.88)$
	=	$100 - 69.43$
	=	30.57
and Outer Rangebet	=	$100 - 1.0 \times (4.24 + 19.5)$
	=	$100 - 23.74$
	=	76.26
Eachway Rangebet	=	$(30.57 + 76.26) / 2$
	=	<u>53.415</u>

3. The $99.50 upbet is worth 49.88 therefore the underlying is at $99.50.

4. The trader has bought this eachway rangebet with the underlying on the uppermost of the two inner strikes which is where the eachway rangebet's delta is at its most negative. Therefore the trader has gone short deltas.

5. The marketmaker has sold the eachway rangebet where the delta is negative. Selling being the same as multiplying a position by –1 means that since a negative (sell) multiplied by a negative (delta) makes a positive, the marketmaker will need to sell the underlying to get delta neutral.

6. The underlying is now midway between the inner strikes where the vega is at its most negative assuming there is not too much time to expiry. Selling the eachway rangebet therefore provides the trader with an attractive position should implied volatility rise. But even should implied volatility not rise, providing the underlying does become more volatile and moves away from the centre of the inner strikes it is likely to prove a winning position.

7. Theta can be at its most positive when the underlying is just inside one of the two inner strikes so the position may be the correct position for the trader to accrue time value. The risk is that the underlying will creep up and through the $99.50 strike where the theta may become extremely negative meaning the trader's strategy is reduced to ruins as his long eachway rangebet decreases in value over time.

Section III:

The previous chapters have been concerned with providing the reader with a theoretical grounding in binary options. The tools of the trade of a proficient options trader are the evaluation of the 'fair' price of an option and understanding how the 'greeks' work under different circumstances. Section III consists of two chapters covering the trading and hedging of binaries.

Firstly Chapter 9 provides guidance on how best to use binaries so the trader can confidently enter a position in order to back a particular market view. The view maybe that the underlying market is going to fall, that the volatility of the underlying is going to rise, or that there is no strong view at all and that the trader simply wants to buy or sell some options for the purpose of taking in time decay.

Chapter 10 covers hedging with different instruments in order that a trader who has already established a position can confidently trade around it. Risk management and the hedging of positions is of prime importance as the ability to efficiently apply different instruments to a book in order to hedge positions can increase the trader's returns dramatically.

9

Trading Binaries

9.0 Introduction

Futures, currencies, stocks, commodities and bonds, i.e. any instrument that has the characteristic of a straight 45° profit and loss line, permit the speculator to do just one thing and that is take a view on the direction of the instrument…fairly tedious really, they might more appropriately be called blunt instruments! Binaries, on the other hand, not only permit the trader to take a view on the direction but to do so with more or less gearing than offered by the linear P&L instruments. Furthermore binaries can also be used to take a view on implied volatility although these instruments are not ideal for this purpose. And finally, if the trader has neither a strong view on either the future direction or volatility, by selling out-of-the-money upbets and downbets the trader can make a profit even if the underlying rises or falls provided it remains below the upbet strike and above the downbet strike. And most importantly of all, binaries have a built-in 'stop'.

The first part of this chapter will explore different ways to take advantage of a directional view using the different binaries previously discussed. Should upbets be bought or downbets sold? Should an eachwaybet be used? Which expiry would be most attractive?

The next section on volatility determines how best to back a view on future market volatility. Should rangebets be sold or upbets and downbets bought? Volatility skew is introduced as a concept which can provide positive input into trading strategies.

Finally, for the passive premium seller who solely wants to 'do a Lloyds of London number' and write premium, which expiry and which strikes does the trader sell, or if a rangebet, buy?

9.1 Directional Trading

Binaries offer a variety of ways to get long or short the underlying. If a trader is bullish of the underlying he requires a positive delta, if bearish a negative delta, which can be achieved by using upbets, downbets and eachwaybets as in Table 9.1.1.

	Upbet	Downbet	Eachwaybet	Rangebet
Long Delta	Buy	Sell	Buy	?
Short Delta	Sell	Buy	Sell	?

Table 9.1.1

The rangebet and eachway rangebet also provide a means by which to get long or short although this is dependent on where the underlying is in relation to the strikes.

If one is bullish one should get long an upbet, short a downbet or long an eachwaybet. Since being long the $100 strike upbet is identical to being short the $100 strike downbet, the choice is now whittled down to:

1. which upbet strike;
2. which expiry;

and if an eachwaybet is to be involved,

1. which strikes;
2. and which expiry.

9.1.1 The Choice of Strike

If the price of a share is $100 (no yield and zero interest rates both spot and forward) and a trader believes it will be higher after the announcement of the company's results in five days, how does one choose between which strikes to buy? Table 9.1.2 lists three different strike upbets with the prices they are on offer at, plus the return a winning bet provides at that price.

Underlying	Strike	Price	Winning Return
$100.00	$100.00	50	100%
	$100.50	25	300%
	$101.00	15	567%

Table 9.1.2

The possible profit and loss for each upbet is illustrated in Fig 9.1.1.

The $100 strike is at-the-money and is worth 50. The cost of the premium is the most expensive and the profit is restricted to 50, but this is offset by the fact that it only has to move upwards by the narrowest of increments for this upbet to win and generate a 100% return. The $100.50 and $101 strikes are only going to cost 25 and 15 respectively with a much higher profit potential of 300% and 567%. The $100.50 and $101 strikes have to see the share increase in value by half of 1% and 1% respectively in just five days.

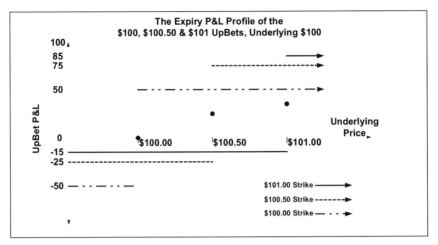

Figure 9.1.1

There is in fact no 'correct' strike to buy as the trader's attitude towards risk and the bullishness of the trader (which only the trader can know) are the most important factors when determining which strike the trader should buy.

The same criteria apply when determining the downbet strike. Table 9.1.3 incorporates a deep in-the-money, an at-the-money and a far out-of-the-money to illustrate different profit profiles and how they each could attract different bettors with different attitudes towards risk. The profit profiles are illustrated in Fig 9.1.2.

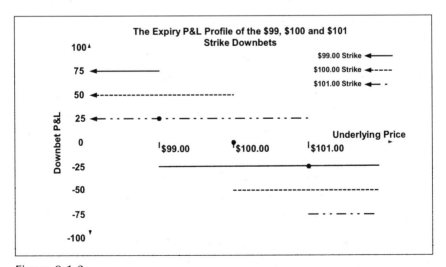

Figure 9.1.2

Underlying	Strike	Price	Winning Return
$100.00	$99.00	25	300%
	$100.00	50	100%
	$101.00	75	33%

Table 9.1.3

Trader A pays 75 for the $101 strike downbet and 'owns' a P&L described by the dot-dash profile. Should the underlying remain below $101 then the downbet will increase in value from 75 to 100 where A makes a profit of 25. Trader B (dotted profile) believes there is a better than an evens money chance that the share will fall by expiry. The downbet is actually offered at 50 which represents a good value bet for trader B. Trader C (solid line) is attracted by the $99 strike downbet. He may be genuinely very bearish of the stock, and believes that the share will fall by 1% by expiry, or on the other hand may simply be an 'out-and-out' punter that likes the risk/return of a 3/1 (300%) shot.

The comment "better than an evens money chance" in the above paragraph is giving away the answer as to which bet to take. A better than evens money chance means that there is a probability of greater than 50:50, or 50%, that the event will happen. In this case the event is that the underlying will fall from its current price of $100 and Trader B thinks that that there is more than a 50% chance of this. The $100 downbet is available at 50 so this bet is actually a 'value' bet for Trader B since he believes that the price should be above 50 to reflect the "better than evens money chance". Likewise the $99 downbet is on offer at 25 which means that the market is stating that there is less than a 25% chance of the share falling below $99. If Trader C also happens to believe that the probability of the share falling below $99 is 25% then this price represents 'fair value' to Trader C; on the other hand if Trader C believes that the probability is 26% or more, then the downbet at 25 is cheap and Trader C also has achieved his 'value bet'.

There is no de facto right or wrong strike to buy since it is an individualistic value judgement based on the trader's (very often subliminal) assessment of probability.

Eachwaybets also offer the trader the opportunity to get long the market but in this case the payoff is not so 'hit and miss'.

Table 9.1.4 provides the underlying price in the top row and the strikes of the two 100:50:0 eachwaybets in the left-hand column, while the body of the table provides the prices and deltas of the bets. Fig 9.1.3 shows expiry P&Ls for both eachwaybets.

EachWayBets	$98.50	$99.25	$100.00	$100.75	$101.50
$99/$101 Price	19.0	33.5	50.0	66.5	81.0
Delta	0.17	0.21	0.23	0.21	0.16
$100/$101 Price	8.0	19.0	36.0	57.0	76.0
Delta	0.06	0.19	0.27	0.28	0.22

Table 9.1.4

The $100/$101 eachwaybet has greater gearing (as measured by the delta) than the $99/$101 bet although it has to initially travel a full point more to achieve it. From the underlying at $98.50, the $99/$101 bet requires the underlying to only travel $0.50 before the bet is worth 50 at expiry to generate a 163% profit and therefore is arguably less risky than the $100/$101 eachway bet that has to travel a full $1.50 to make a profit at expiry, although the 'less risky' bet requires an initial outlay of 19 versus 8.

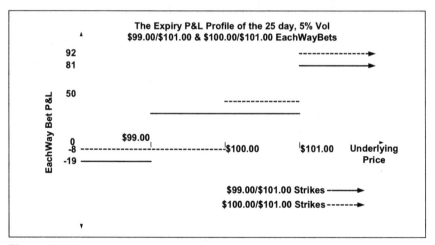

Figure 9.1.3

Yet again the choice between the above two profiles (and many others that would be available) is a very personal matter as the individual's attitude towards risk plus the confidence they hold in their view on the underlying price all combine to render 'rules' obsolete.

It is possible though to once again identify 'the value bet' when considering which eachwaybet to trade. If in the above example the underlying is trading at $99.25 and the $99/$101 eachwaybet is trading at 34 and the $100/$101 eachwaybet is trading at 22, to evaluate the fair value the trader needs to assess the probability of the underlying being above $99, $100 and $101. After pondering the trader reckons the odds at 60%, 30% and 10% for the underlying to be above $99, $100 and $101 respectively. Referring to eachwaybet evaluation from Chapter 7, Section 7.2, the eachwaybets should be worth:

$99.00/$101.00   = $(10 - (100 - 60) + 100) / 2$

                                 =   35

$100.00/$101.00   = $(10 - (100 - 30) + 100) / 2$

                                 =   20

and when comparing these values to what is available in the market the 34 offer for the $99/$101 eachwaybet looks good value compared to the 22 offer for the $100/$101 eachwaybet.

Finally, the rangebet and the eachway rangebet present an interesting means of getting long or short. Although this analysis concentrates on the rangebet it applies equally well to the eachway rangebet. Table 9.1.5 provides three prices for the $99/$101 rangebets assuming the underlying at $98.75, $100 and $101.25 with the deltas in the row underneath.

	$98.75	$100.00	$101.25
Price	31	50	31
Delta	+0.25	0	−0.25

Table 9.1.5

By buying a rangebet with the underlying lower than the centre of the rangebet, in this case $100 and, assuming time and volatility haven't driven the deltas to zero, the delta will be positive. Therefore, with the underlying below the lower strike of $99, going long a rangebet is bullish of the underlying, while selling the rangebet creates a short position in the underlying. At $101 the opposite applies.

If one held a long position in the above $99/$101 rangebet with the underlying at $98.75, and then the underlying rallies to $100, the rangebet would then have a delta of zero. Therefore this directional view is 'long' only during a $1.25 upward move. If the underlying keeps travelling upwards through $100, the bullish trader now owns a short position as the deltas are now negative, and the position is working against his view. This is a trade that needs a lot of monitoring, preferably with the exit strategy considered on entering into the position. The trader may well decide to sell the rangebet at 50 and take a profit of 19.

9.1.2 The Choice of Expiry

There is nothing more irritating than having been long a boat-load of teenies (out-of-the-money options with very little or no value) and seeing the underlying whip upwards or downwards through the strike the day after they've expired. Alternatively nothing is more rewarding than holding them and seeing them explode in value on the last day. Timing's everything.

When placing a bet on the future move in a financial or a commodity it is not enough to just forecast a move up or down. The binary trader must also have a clear view as to when the move might take place. In Section 9.1.1 the trader took the view that the company's results were going to be the trigger for the move, therefore taking a position in a bet that expired prior to the results would be a rather unrewarding ploy. If there is an event that one feels will propel the underlying in one direction or another then that event must occur within the life of the option. Simple you imagine? I wonder how many non-bond equity options traders realise that the Sep 10 yr Notes expire in August?

The impact of different events will influence the price of instruments for different lengths of time following the event. Events such as central bank action on short-term rates will have an immediate and usually finite effect on the front month eurodollar and Euribor futures and any other contract that is implicitly related to the central bank's rate. The back month 'dollars' and 'bor' will likely be influenced over a lengthier time span as the market digests longer term implications. It may be that if the central bank raised rates it might be construed as the bottom of a ten-year cyclical decline in rates and for the bond market it may signal the start of a long-term decline in bond prices. Therefore choosing a bet that has a longer time to expiry subsequent to the event may make more sense for instruments such as bonds while choosing an expiry date that closely follows the event may well provide better gearing for events such as changes in central bank rates. The CBOT's Fed Funds binary options expire the day after the FOMC meeting.

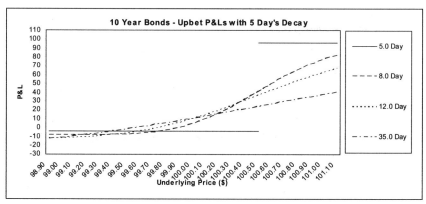

Figure 9.1.4

Fig 9.1.4 illustrates possible P&L profiles available on a Monday morning for a trader who wants to be long 10-year bonds over the Friday US unemployment number via the binary market. On Monday morning, with the bonds at $99.50, the 5, 8, 12 and 35-day $100.50 upbets are valued at 4.35, 8.78, 13.40 and 25.67 respectively.

		Bond Prices				
Days	Cost	$99.00	$99.50	$100.00	$100.50	$101.00
5	4.35	0.00	0.00	0.00	50.00	100.00
8	8.78	0.05	1.36	13.51	49.91	86.27
12	13.40	1.48	7.39	23.46	49.86	76.22
35	25.67	14.54	24.05	36.13	49.71	63.27

Table 9.1.6

Table 9.1.6 provides the values of the upbets on Friday's close with five days less of time value and unchanged implied volatility so that the 5-day bet has expired and the 8, 12 and 35-day bets have 3, 7 and 30 days left to expiry. The maximum downside of the 5-day bet is 4.35, yet if the bonds settle at $100.51 the bet will be worth 100 returning a 2,199% profit. The 35-day bet provides a further month for the bet to come good and allow the bonds to settle above $100.50. There is less risk involved. Or is there? The maximum loss is now 25.67, an increase in maximum downside of 21.32. Furthermore, if the bonds close at $100.51 on Friday the upbet will be worth 50 providing a return of just 95%. Yet at $100.49 the 35-day upbet is now worth 49.49, a profit of 92.8%, and is still in with a shout of being worth 100. The 5-day bet is worth zero at $100.49 and has no further potential; it has expired.

On choosing the expiry in the above example the trader has to consider how confident he is in getting the $1 rally by Friday night. If very confident the trader should go for the gearing and take the five day expiry. If the trader thinks it may take longer then he should give himself more elbow room and go for a longer expiry. The bet will cost more but the trader can console himself by considering that the extra cost is the cost of insurance against the bonds finishing at $100.49.

Yet again there is no right or wrong expiry as the choice is very much dependent on the risk profile the trader is comfortable with, and providing the trader has a good understanding of the P&L profiles on offer, only the trader will be aware of his comfort zone.

9.2   Trading Volatility

This section covers the concept of taking binary options positions because the trader considers the implied volatility of the options is too low or too high. The trader may consider that:

1. Implied volatility is out of line with historical volatility;

2. Implied volatility will change owing to external factors; or

3. Implied volatility of a particular bet is out of line with other bets of the same series.

The general rule with these sorts of positions is that since the trader is taking a view on implied volatility and not on the future direction of the underlying then the position should be instigated as a delta neutral strategy. It would be a frustrated trader indeed who has bought 'cheap' upbets and seen implied volatility rise but lost money because the position was not delta neutral and the underlying has fallen.

9.2.1   Implied Volatility v Historic Volatility

Fig 9.2.1 illustrates the 20-day and 50-day historic volatility for a currency pair going back two years. It also provides the implied volatility for a conventional option series. This implied volatility will always be taken as the at-the-money option since this is the strike which is most sensitive to changes in implied volatility and as it always has the most time value. Is it possible to draw similar conclusions when applied to binary option trading? The answer, unfortunately, is a resounding "No".

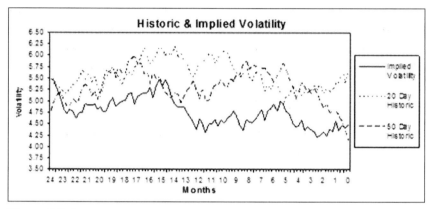

Figure 9.2.1

On referring back to Chapter 3, Fig 3.6.1, one can see that as implied volatility rises the peak of volatility moves away from the at-the-money. The peak of volatility moves towards the at-the-money over time. This means that evaluating the implied volatility of a binary over a two-year period as in Fig 9.2.1 becomes problematical as the relevant strike changes over time and comparable data is difficult to establish. In itself this could well be a show-stopper when attempting to buy 'cheap' premium on the back of a historical volatility measure.

But just suppose a series of binaries has been identified as cheap compared to historical volatility; now the problem of choosing the bet to take advantage of the anomaly has to be overcome. If implied is cheap (compared to historic) in conventional terms the solution is easy, buy the at-the-money straddle; but with binaries the at-the-money straddle (or any other binary straddle for that matter) is always worth 100. With binaries one would need to buy the out-of-the-money upbet or downbet and respectively sell or buy the underlying to get delta neutral. Just say the long upbet and short underlying is the trade executed and that the trader calls it right and implied volatility rises. Table 9.2.1 illustrates upbet prices over a rise in volatility along with the P&L.

		Underlying				
		$99.50	$99.75	$100.00	$100.25	$100.50
Imp	Upbet	26.90	37.84	49.84	61.82	72.73
Vol	Delta	0.40	0.47	0.49	0.46	0.40
7%	Vega	2.87	1.64	−0.02	−1.68	−2.91
	P&L	+$9,060	+$4,500	+$1,000	−$2,520	−$7,110
Imp	Upbet	23.66	35.94	49.86	63.76	76.01
Vol	Delta	0.44	0.53	0.57	0.53	0.44
6%	Vega	3.65	2.20	−0.02	−2.24	−3.70
	P&L	+$5,820	+$2,600	+$1,020	−$580	−$3,830
Imp	Upbet	19.50	33.34	49.88	66.41	80.22
Vol	Delta	0.47	0.62	0.68	0.62	0.47
5%	Vega	4.71	3.09	−0.02	−3.13	−4.76
	P&L	+$1,660	0	+$1,040	+$2,070	+$380

Table 9.2.1

In the table the upbet, delta, vega and P&L are displayed across five underlying prices with implied volatility increasing from 5% to 7%. The strike price is $100 with the underlying initially assumed at $99.75 where the trade was initiated, so that the $100 is out-of-the-money and therefore has a positive vega. As volatility rises from 5% to 6% and 7%, the upbet will therefore increase in value for an unchanged underlying. At 5% the delta of the $100 upbet is 0.62 so against an assumed position of $1,000 per point of upbets bought, $620 of the underlying needs to be sold in order to be delta neutral.

So long as the underlying remains below $100, the vega of the upbet remains positive and the rationale of the choice of strike remains intact. But a problem arises if the underlying rises through the strike so that the upbet chosen is now in-the-money and the vega has become increasingly negative. The initial vega of +3.09 at $99.75 has become −4.76 at $100.50. At $100.50 and 5% volatility the position makes a profit of $380 solely down to the effect of gamma. At $99.75 the $1000/pt upbet is offset by $620/pt of the underlying. As the underlying travels to $100 the positive gamma means that at $100 the position has a long delta of $60 per point since the delta at the underlying of $100 has increased to 0.68. At $100.25 the delta is back down to 0.62 as the upbet is in-the-money and now has a negative gamma. For the whole 50-tick move from $99.75 to $100.25, the position is long the underlying so that at $100.25 a profit of $2,070 is made. At $100.50 the delta of the position is now −$150 per point and the profit has been reduced to $380. But this profit is all luck; the trader put the position on because he thought that implied volatility would rise and it hasn't done so; it is still 5%.

Now at $100.50, if the implied volatility does rise as the trader initially forecast and established the position for, then the position is actually going to lose money, i.e. −$3,830 at 6% and −$7,110 at 7%. This risk reversal, as it is known, is common throughout binary options and there is little to be done about it; it is the nature of the beast. An instrument that switches character to provide the trader with the opposite P&L scenario to the one required could be considered at best fickle, at worst a downright liability.

In effect, trading binaries against historic volatility is a non-starter as:

1. There is a problem generating comparable implied volatilities over time as the strike used needs to be shifted closer to the underlying.

2. A similar problem exists when attempting to generate comparable implied volatilities as changing implied volatilities also necessitate an adjustment of the strike to use.

3. And if these problems were overcome then the risk reversal means that if the underlying passed through the strike the position is working in exactly the opposite manner as intended.

9.2.2 External Factors & Implied Volatility

If one believes that implied volatility may rise because of a change in external factors, e.g. economic data or political uncertainty, the same problems will exist as in the section on historic v implied volatility. Binaries are certainly not the most effective instrument therefore to take advantage of the trader's correct views on future implied volatility.

9.2.3 Bets v Bets (of same series)

'Volatility skew' (or 'volatility smile') is the implied volatility differential across a range of strikes in one series. The usual incidence of skew is for out-of-the-money calls to trade at an implied volatility lower than the at-the-money options and for out-of-the-money puts to have an implied volatility at a premium to the at-the-monies.

If the assumptions underpinning the Black-Scholes theory were true, then it is a matter of conjecture as to whether skew would exist. So how does one explain the existence of skew? The obvious explanation is that the lognormal distribution carries little weight amongst the options trading community. Indeed there are mathematical models, e.g. specific trinomial models, which are capable of adopting parameters generating prices in line with a symmetrical standard normal distribution, the bell-shaped distribution.

Another view may be that as markets rise, market participants become complacent as a feelgood factor sets in. Those that aren't long will just kick themselves for having 'missed the boat' while those of whom are long feel they do not need to hedge against upward moves. In contrast when markets 'go into reverse' the rate of decline can engender panic. Fund managers scramble to unwind long positions, thereby exacerbating swings in the market. Others cover by buying puts, sometimes at any price. In the experience of the author options marketmakers generally make more money in falling markets than in rising markets simply because the number of irrational panic trades increases as markets go into steep decline. This (non-mathematical) scenario is the one the author would promote in explaining why 'skew' exists. Ultimately, how many people insure against their house going up in value? Everybody insures against their house going up in smoke!

Fig 9.2.2 shows a scatter diagram with each point reflecting the implied volatility at any one moment of bids and offers of upbets and downbets with an underlying of $18.

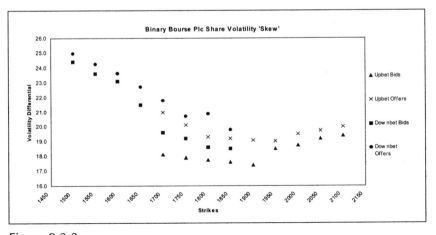

Figure 9.2.2

There are no prices for deep in-the-money options as marketmakers generally offer prices in out-of-the-monies since this is where the majority of the business takes place. By taking the average of the two or four points one achieves an arithmetic mean of the implied volatility.

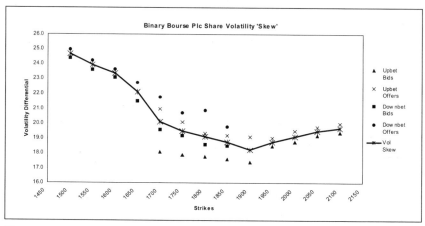

Figure 9.2.3

This is added to the diagram in Fig 9.2.3, where one can discern a rather irregular curve with points that appear to be out of line with other points. Using a manual method or a 'smoothing' tool such as a cubic spline one can achieve a smooth line such as that in Fig 9.2.4.

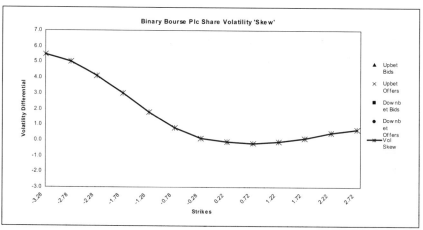

Figure 9.2.4

This smoothed curve in is the graphical representation of the volatility skew and would be used to make adjustments to the inputted volatility when generating fair values. Once the skew has been established the curve 'slides' with both volatility and the underlying so that the relationship of a strike to the underlying becomes an absolute variable. Should the underlying be trading at $18, then the implied volatility to add or subtract from the base volatility would be zero.

If the underlying now rises by 50¢ to $18.50 then the implied volatility of the $18 would be the base level volatility plus the volatility increment of the $17.50 strike. The base level of volatility is the flat rate implied volatility that most accurately reflects that volatility close to the underlying. If the underlying had only risen 28¢ to $18.28 the implied volatility of the $18 strike would be the base level volatility plus:

$$\text{(Vol at \$18.00 - Vol at \$18.50)} \times \text{(Underlying -} \\ \$18.00)/(\$18.50 - \$18.00)$$

Therefore if the volatility skew determines that the $18.50 strike trades 0.5% below the $18 strike, and if the base level volatility is 19%, then the adjusted implied volatility of the $18 strike at the underlying of $18.28 is now:

$$19\% + \{0.5\% \times \$0.28/\$0.5\} = 19.28\%$$

Drawing straight line interpolations between strikes is an overly simplistic method of calculating the skew. The more strikes that are introduced the shorter the distance between the strikes which in turn creates greater accuracy. Taking the inclusion of strikes to the extreme, i.e. one notional strike per underlying increment, tends to the methodology of the cubic spline which creates smooth curves of the 'best fit'.

Once the skew has been modelled accurately to the trader's satisfaction, the fair values of a range of upbets and downbets can be established over a range of the underlying. Each bet requires an implied volatility input derived from the skew to evaluate the fair value. If the market price for a downbet shows a bid higher than the fair value then this may indicate a sale. Should a different downbet of the same series now be offered at less than the fair value, the trader trading the skew now has put the binary put spread on at a credit to fair value.

The assessment the trader has to make immediately after the first downbet bid has entered the market and is higher than the fair value is: 1) is my overall volatility too low, and/or 2) is my volatility skew accurate. As soon as the 'cheap' offer of the second downbet is entered into the market the first problem can be discarded; overall implied volatility is not too low.

The skew may still be inaccurate though, although it is more likely that the spread is probably 'a do' providing enough diligence was spent in getting the skew correct in the first place.

The trading of the skew in this manner is primarily the preserve of the binary and conventional options marketmaker.

9.3 Selling Time

The risk reversal problem associated with entering into volatility trades rears its head again for the binary trader selling premium in order to 'take in time value'. If the out-of-the-money upbet seller thinks that selling upbets has to be more advantageous than the equivalent conventional sale of out-of-the-money calls because of the limited risk in shorting binaries, then think again. The theta of the upbet and downbet changes signs as the underlying travels through the strike, so should the out-of-the-money upbet seller who is long the underlying in a delta neutral manner see his short option become in-the-money, then he now has a short option increasing in value over time.

9.4 Summary

A binary is probably a more dextrous instrument than a conventional option when used solely for the purpose of speculating on the price of the underlying. The binary can create more or less gearing than a conventional bond, stock, currency or any other future or option, all in a limited-risk manner.

Those traders that are looking to buy or sell volatility or sell time decay should probably concentrate on using conventional options. The risk reversal inherent in the binary position renders bets as far from ideal in exploiting views on volatility or time decay.

9.5 Exercises

1. On the London Stock Exchange Vodafone is trading at £1.50. A trader has a strong view of an imminent upward move in the stock and wishes to get 'geared up'. The following quotes are available:

Upbets	Strike		
Days to Expiry	£1.40	£1.50	£1.60
10	87.0	50	12.4
30	80.0	50	19.2

What could he/she do?

2. In Hong Kong Hutchison Whampoa is trading at HK$77.10/ HK$77.30. A speculator fancies some bad news in the next figures and strongly expects that at the expiry of the September binary options the stock will be trading in the range HK$70–HK$72. The speculator has HK$10,000 to invest and wishes to maximise his potential profit in accordance with this view. The following binary options are available in the market with associated prices:

Sep Binaries	Strikes	Price
Downbet	HK$71.00	13.7
Downbet	HK$72.00	18.3
Eachway Downbet (100:50:0)	HK$72.00/HK$74.00	17.8
Eachway Downbet (100:40:0)	HK$70.00/HK$72.00	7.5
Rangebet	HK$70.00/HK$72.00	7.09
Eachway Rangebet	HK$68.00/HK$70.00/HK$72.00/HK$74.00	14.8

What should he/she do?

9.6 Answers

1. The key words in the question are 'imminent' and 'geared up'. Imminent implies that the trader should choose a bet with nearest expiry since bets with nearest expiry have the least time value and therefore the greatest gearing. The further the out-of-the-money strike the greater the gearing so in this case the bettor should choose to buy the £1.60 upbet at 12.4.

2. Start by calculating the winnings for each bet if the speculator is correct and the underlying finishes between HK$70 and HK$72.

The return on the first downbet is (100–13.7)/13.7 = 6.3 returning a profit of $6,300 if the underlying is below HK$71. But if the underlying is between HK$71 and HK$72 the bet loses and the punter loses HK$1,000.

The return on the second downbet is (100–18.3)/18.3 = 4.47 returning a profit of HK$4,470.

The HK$72/HK$74 eachway downbet returns (100–17.8)/17.8 = 4.62 returning a profit of HK$4,620.

This eachway downbet is only worth 40 between the strikes so the return is (40–7.5)/7.5 = 4.33 returning $4,333 between HK$70 and HK$72.

The rangebet returns (100–7.09)/7.09 = 13.1 returning HK$13,100.

The eachway rangebet returns (100–14.8)/14.8 = 5.76 returning $5,760.

Clearly the best bet for this punter is buying the HK$70/HK$72 rangebet for 7.09 generating a profit of HK$13,100.

10

Hedging Binaries

10.0 Introduction

In this day and age one may be excused in being rather confused as to what is and is not a hedge based on the activities of so-called 'hedge funds'. If ever the nomenclature of a financial market operator was misapplied then this is it. Travelling back through the years it is possible to highlight hedge funds that were 'hedging' one country's government bonds against a different government's bonds on the basis that yields were misaligned. Views were based on theoretical concepts such as purchasing price parity, cost of living indices, et al, determining theoretical bond yields and thereby supposedly providing hedge funds with profit generating opportunities. The losses incurred by one infamous fund that 'blew out' in this manner confound the notion that any form of hedge was in operation at all.

More recently hedge funds are taking sizeable positions in individual companies' equity in order to pressurise those companies' boards to change their corporate strategy or philosophy, or even simply to reimburse shareholders with a special dividend payment. Extraordinarily the German Deutsche Börse itself had to submit to such an attack and abandon its attempt to launch a costly hostile bid for the London Stock Exchange.

Nowadays it is generally accepted by investors in hedge funds that they are very often putting their money into a 'punting' fund and backing the fund's trading ability to predetermine market movements. Hedging when discussed in this book is the boring, old-fashioned, traditional concept involving reducing the risk inherent in an open position.

Although binaries can provide the ideal speculating instrument this section will describe and analyse hedging binaries with the underlying, with conventional options and with other binaries.

Hedging itself is an art. If a trader is long 100 Microsoft shares and he wants a 100% hedge then simple, sell 100 Microsoft shares. Hedging options of any sort though is not so 'black and white'. This section on hedging will concentrate on delta hedging, i.e. the exposure of a binary or a portfolio of binaries to a movement in the underlying. The hedging of vega and theta will also be cursorily addressed but owing to the upbet having both positive and negative vegas and thetas dependent on whether the upbet is in the money or not, fewer hard and fast rules can be set when attempting to hedge these particular greeks.

10.1 Binaries as Call Spreads

Starting off this section on hedging binaries by analysing the hedging of binaries with conventional options may seem an odd choice. Maybe binaries with binaries would be more appropriate? What this section will show is that for a particular instant in time a combination of conventional options provide an exact 100% hedge, but only for one instant in time. Through establishing the behaviour and attributes of the binary in this manner it is hoped that the whole concept of binary hedging, certainly for the conventional options trader, will become a great deal more intuitive.

10.1.1 The Binary as a Conventional Call Spread

At any moment in time the profit and loss profile of a binary can be exactly replicated by a conventional call spread. The theta of the binary means that the strikes of the conventional have to continually move towards each other to maintain this state. Figs 10.1.1 to 10.1.4 illustrate this relationship and show how over time the hedge becomes increasingly inefficient as both profiles approach zero time to expiry. Fig 10.1.1 offers the 10-day profiles of the $100 upbet and the $99.50/$100.50 conventional call spread, which entails a long position in a $99.50 call and a short position in a $100.50 call. Clearly with ten days to go the call spread price maps almost exactly onto the upbet price over a range of underlying prices. When there are more than 10 days to expiry the profiles become identical and therefore a perfect hedge. Fig 10.1.2 shows the relationship with only one day left to expiry. Although there is now 'daylight' between the profiles, a conventional call spread might still be considered an efficient hedge. Fig 10.1.3 shows a marked change in the separate profiles and the use of a call spread as a hedge becomes tenuous, while Fig 10.1.4 presents the profiles at expiry.

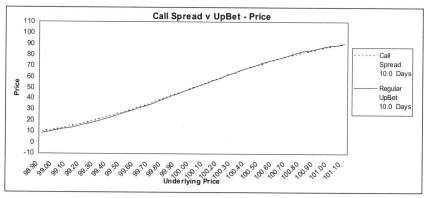

Figure 10.1.1

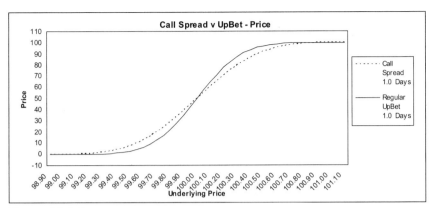

Figure 10.1.2

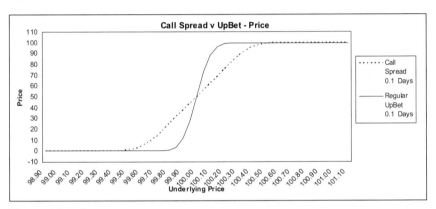

Figure 10.1.3

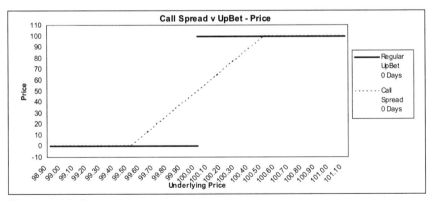

Figure 10.1.4

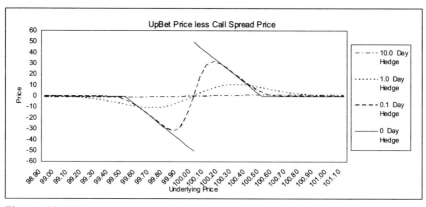

Figure 10.1.5

Fig 10.1.5 illustrates the discrepancies over time between the upbet and the call spread. For a call spread to be an efficient hedge, then the difference between the call spread and the upbet needs to be zero for any underlying. From Fig 10.1.5 the horizontal line at price zero reflects the almost 100% efficiency of the 10-day upbet/call spread hedge, while the hedge at expiry has become ineffectual. The reason the call spread is so ineffectual at expiry can be explained thus: the $100 upbet has one second left to expiry, the underlying is exactly on the strike so the upbet is therefore worth 50. The call spread on the same underlying has exactly the same scenario with one second to expiry meaning the call spread is also worth 50. In the last second the underlying moves up 1¢ to $100.01 so the upbet 'wins' and is worth 100. The call spread is now worth 50.01. If on the other hand the underlying had fallen 1¢ and the upbet owner had hedged by selling the call spread the portfolio would lose 49.99 since the price of the upbet has fallen from 50 to 0 while the call spread has fallen from 50 to 49.99. A 1¢ move in the underlying with one second to expiry would therefore require one upbet to be hedged with 50 / 1 = 50 call spreads. A 10¢ move would require the upbet/call spread ratio to be 1:5. Using call spreads to hedge in such a manner is therefore impractical as the portfolio would need a constant reappraisal and adjustment of how many call spreads are required.

The impracticalities of hedging with call spreads is highlighted by the fact that this methodology requires an infinite number of different call spreads with strike prices equidistant around the upbet strike price.

This analysis has not been submitted as the solution to the hedging conundrum that besets binaries but more as a warning. There are no easy solutions to hedging binaries and any conventional options traders who have tried to hedge a call or put spread will now be aware of the fundamental problems in hedging binaries. This does not mean that the hedging of binaries is a non-starter since hedging with some instruments can create even greater profit-making opportunities, the most profitable being covered in the section after next.

10.2 Hedging with the Underlying
10.2.1 Introduction

Usually the underlying is the first port of call when hedging options as it takes away the immediate directional risk. The virtues of hedging a binary with the underlying are severely limited in that a bet with maximum downside is converted to a position with unlimited downside. Section 10.1 determined that a binary is a call spread in disguise so that anyone with a background in conventional options trading will intuitively recognise the problems in hedging binaries with the underlying.

10.2.2 The Upbet v the Underlying

Fig 10.2.1 illustrates a $10 per point long position in the $100 strike upbet with five days to expiry, a short underlying position, plus the profile of the hedged position.

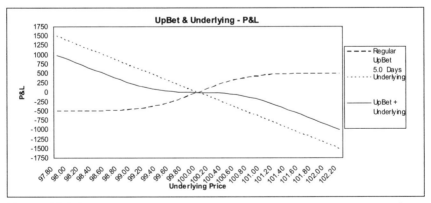

Figure 10.2.1

The boundaries of the upbet P&L are horizontal at ±500. The at-the-money delta at $100 for this 5-day upbet is 0.68 so a short position of $6.80 per point of the underlying is assumed. The aggregate of these two positions is the solid line 'Upbet + Underlying'. The delta neutral hedging has provided the flat P&L profile at the current underlying price of $100 but has at the same time swivelled the upbet profile 68° (although the scale does not reflect this) in a clockwise manner. This has resulted in eliminating directional risk at an underlying of $100 but producing an aggregate P&L with an unlimited loss profile on the upside. As the time to expiry decreases from five days to zero, even if the underlying remains unchanged at $100, the delta will increase necessitating further shorting of the underlying and creating an even greater upside risk.

10.2.3 The Downbet v the Underlying

The downbet, as has been previously impressed upon the reader, is nothing less than the opposite side of the upbet, therefore the analysis for the long 5-day upbet applies equally as well to applying the underlying to hedge the short 5-day downbet. Fig 10.2.2 shows a long 25-day downbet position (or short upbet position) with a long position in the underlying. As expected the absolute delta for the at-the-money downbet is less since there are 25 days to expiry; in this instance the delta is −0.30. Therefore a long position in the underlying of $3 per point is assumed, which is calculated by multiplying the $10 per point of the downbet by the delta of −0.30.

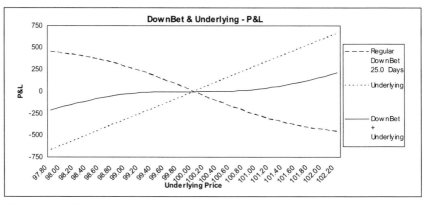

Figure 10.2.2

The aggregate profile shows a maximum loss on the graph extending to less than $250 compared with the $1,000 loss in Fig 10.2.1 so it is possible to conclude that the underlying is a better hedge the longer there is to expiry owing to the lower gamma of the bet, but at the extremes it is still creating risk.

10.2.4 The Rangebet v the Underlying

Hedging the rangebet with the underlying is a pointless exercise if the strikes are too close together as what may require a short underlying position may quickly change to require a long underlying position. As Fig 6.9.1 indicated, the gamma between the strikes is always negative so hedging a long rangebet between the strikes is fraught with danger; as the underlying whips backwards and forwards through the central point between the strikes, guaranteed losses in trading the underlying delta hedge will be forthcoming. If the underlying is trading outside the strikes then there is an argument for delta hedging, but as soon as the underlying moves between the two strikes the above risky scenario appears again.

What can be safely asserted is that yet again hedging this particular binary converts a bet with a limited loss profile into a position with an unlimited loss potential, yet with the rangebet it would be even more difficult to present a rational reason for hedging in the first place.

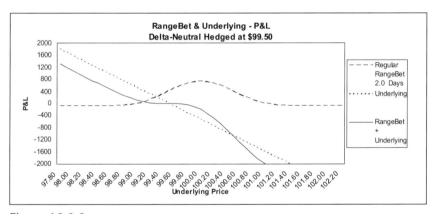

Figure 10.2.3

10.2.5 Summary

Hedging binaries with the underlying creates risk far in excess of the risk it eliminates. If it is necessary to get a hedge on quick then use the underlying but almost immediately look for a hedge involving another binary or conventional option.

10.3 Bets & Conventionals

Hedging binaries with conventional calls and puts is potentially a highly potent hedging strategy. The most obvious reason for using conventional

173

options to hedge with is that they possess gamma and thereby enable the trader to more efficiently tailor the hedge.

10.3.1 Hedging with Conventional Calls

The following diagrams are pairs of charts of (1) long upbets with long conventional calls and (2) short upbets hedged with long conventional calls both over a shortening time to expiry, all with a common strike price of $100 and implied volatility of 5%. The 10-day graph of Fig 10.3.1a shows that the price profiles do not significantly diverge until an underlying of approximately $100.80 is reached while Fig 10.3.1b shows the effect of hedging the same short upbet with the long call. In any market such a risk-reward profile would be highly desirable but as has always been asserted, there is no such thing as a free lunch, and here the downside is that time erodes providing the following less attractive scenarios.

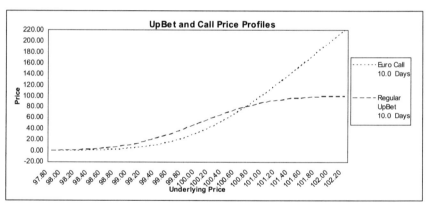

Figure 10.3.1a

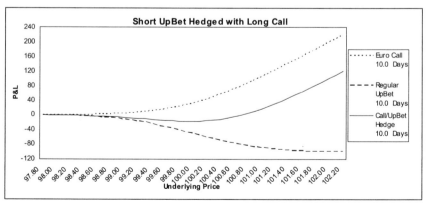

Figure 10.3.1b

Fig 10.3.2a and 10.3.2b show the one day equivalent positions where between the underlying prices of $100 and $101 the individual price profiles are diverging with the consequential dip in the hedge portfolio between the underlying at $100.20 and $100.40.

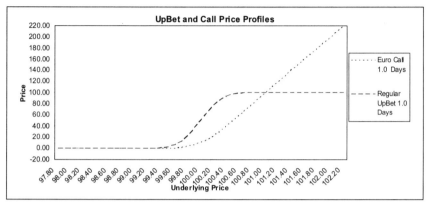

Figure 10.3.2a

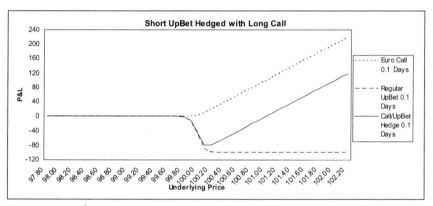

Figure 10.3.2b

This gap becomes more pronounced with 0.1 days to expiry as illustrated by Fig 10.3.3a and 10.3.3b. The definition of the upbet and call expiry profiles is now clearly taking shape.

Finally Fig 10.3.4a and 10.3.4b illustrate the expiry price profiles with the P&L profile of the aggregate position. The hedge profile in Fig 10.3.4b is the same as a conventional call option at expiry except here the 45° upward slope now starts at –100 at the strike. This gap at the underlying gives the alternative name, the gap option, to this combination of long call with short upbet, and vice versa. If the underlying settles at exactly the strike, since it is already assumed that an upbet will settle at 50 (see Section 1.2.2 earlier), in Fig 10.3.4b the loss will actually be 50. As the underlying rises to $101 the P&L becomes zero, and above $101 the hedge portfolio increases in value in a ratio of 1:1 with the underlying like any in-the-money conventional call option. Hedging the binary with a call is a less risky alternative than hedging with the underlying since although a loss of 100 can still be generated if the underlying expires a fraction above the strike, this does prove to be the maximum loss. Fig 10.3.1b reveals that hedging with calls with ten days or more to expiry is a very attractive proposition since the hedge is tantamount to generating a free call option.

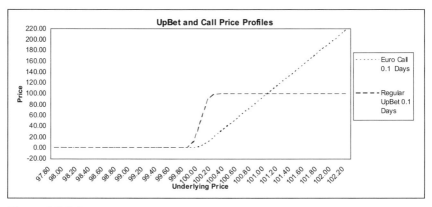

Figure 10.3.3a

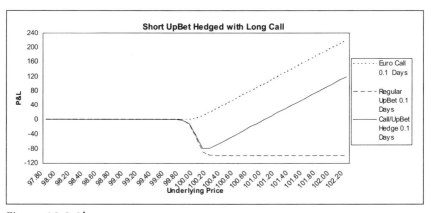

Figure 10.3.3b

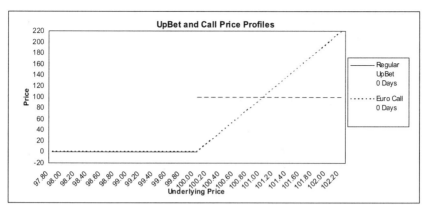

Figure 10.3.4a

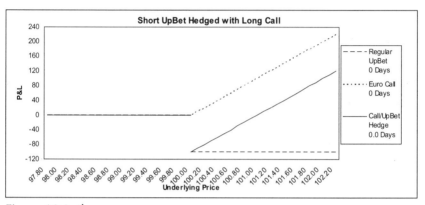

Figure 10.3.4b

Another way of looking at this scenario from the point of view of a conventional options trader is that a 'ladder' or 'Christmas Tree' has been created. A ladder or Tree is a combination of three conventional calls whereby there is a long position in the lowest strike call, followed by a short position in the next highest strike call, followed by another short position in the highest call. The short upbet position in Fig 10.3.4b is made up of a short call spread with strikes equidistant around $100, and to this has been added a long $100 call hence creating a short ladder. A short ladder position (as in Fig 10.3.4b) with the strike of the middle call being at-the-money is a long gamma position.

If in the above example a long upbet is hedged with a short call, then by inverting Fig 10.3.4b it is obvious that the hedge is once again generating risk. Here an instrument with a limited risk profile, the long upbet, is being hedged with an instrument, the short call, that has an unlimited risk profile. This hedge is an even worse alternative than hedging with the underlying since now the hedged portfolio does not reap the rewards of a downward move in the underlying.

10.3.2 Hedging with Puts

The diagrams in the above section have illustrated how a long conventional call can be used to hedge a short upbet. If the short upbet was viewed as a long downbet then clearly conventional calls can be used equally well for hedging in-the-money downbets. It will be left to the reader to consider hedging the out-of-the-money downbet with conventional puts.

10.3.3 Hedging Rangebets with Strangles

Figs 10.3.5 through to Fig 10.3.8 illustrate comparable price profiles of rangebets and strangles. It should be borne in mind that selling a rangebet and buying a strangle is not a hedge. Returning to Section 6.2 it was pointed out that market convention determines that a winning rangebet is one that expires with the underlying between the strikes, a situation comparable with selling the strangle with the same strikes. So when hedging rangebets with strangles it is important to remember that a purchase of a rangebet requires a purchase of the corresponding strangle in order to provide an efficient hedge, and vice versa.

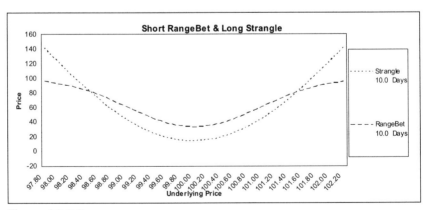

Figure 10.3.5a

On studying Fig 10.3.5a it is apparent that the rangebet is worth slightly more than the strangle between the strikes when there are ten days to expiry. Fig 10.3.5b provides an attractive profile whereby one receives a

178

credit for taking a position that can only make money as the underlying moves away from the strikes.

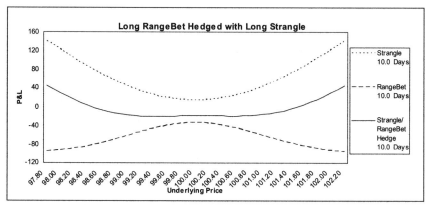

Figure 10.3.5b

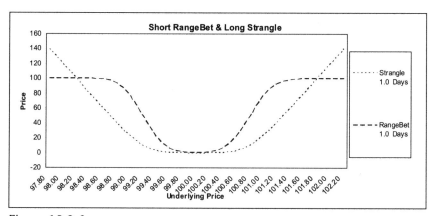

Figure 10.3.6a

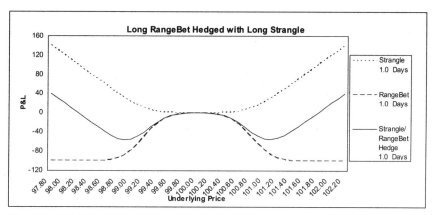

Figure 10.3.6b

Fig 10.3.6 show that with one day to expiry this position is proving to be more risky outside either of the two strikes. But as the underlying moves away from the strikes the long strangle position dominates with the ±45° profile.

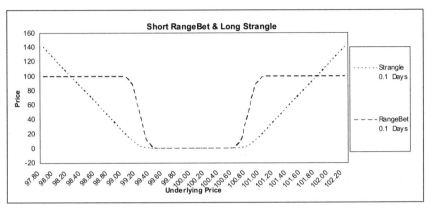

Figure 10.3.7a

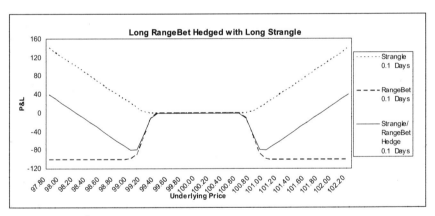

Figure 10.3.7b

With 0.1 day to expiry the hedged position now has a downside of –80, while the expiry position of Fig 10.3.8 shows a settlement price of –100 in two places. What is illustrated by the graphs is how options can provide an excellent hedge with ten days to expiry and it may even be considered that the hedge 'works' up to the last day prior to expiry. The hedge only really falls apart with less than one day to expiry when there is little correlation in prices below and above the strikes.

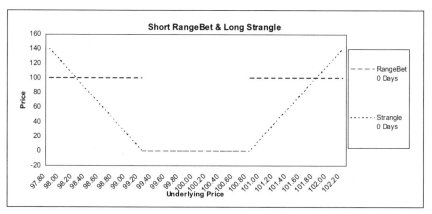

Figure 10.3.8a

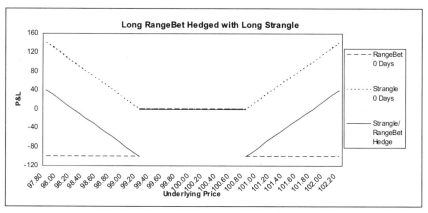

Figure 10.3.8b

For a binary option marketmaker who is constantly looking to 'hedge out' risk, this inability to hedge with the most natural of alternatives to binaries on the final day to expiry leaves him/her with the option of reducing the position as much as possible and then 'taking a flyer' as the only available strategy left. But then again this is the stark choice options marketmakers have in general as gammas start escalating, creating major problems with delta management. At least the binary options marketmaker has the luxury that although an at-the-money bet at expiry becomes unhedgeable, at least the downside is known and 'capped'. This cannot be said of conventional options marketmakers who find themselves short premium, short gamma with an underlying whipping backward and forward through the strike. The author knows a number of conventional options marketmakers whom have been 'carried out' (gone bust) in this manner on the day of expiry.

10.3.4 Summary

The non-linear nature of conventional options offer better hedges for bets than the underlying; indeed with enough time to expiry the correlation between an option and a bet is particularly high.

It is undesirable (from a delta viewpoint) to hedge long upbets and downbets (and short rangebets) with short conventional options positions owing to the unlimited exposure to loss such a hedge creates.

From a marketmaker's perspective running a binary book from the short premium side and hedging with long options may well be a lucrative objective since the position will generally offer a cheap long gamma play.

10.4   Hedging Bets with Bets

The fact that a long upbet is the same as a short downbet, plus any combination of bets generates a limited downside scenario, in many respects trivialises the concept of hedging of bets with bets. This section analyses the hedges on offer and how they may be fruitfully employed.

10.4.1 Long Upbet Hedged with Short Upbet

Since an upbet can be viewed as a conventional call spread, hedging a binary with a binary could be viewed as generating a strategy that is similar to a conventional condor/butterfly. Hedging binaries in this manner creates greater upside risk if the higher strike binary is traded in the same lot size/dollar amount per point as the lower binary strike. The nearer out-of-the-money binary has lower gearing than the further out-of-the-money therefore going long the nearer and shorting the further creates a negative P&L above the upper strike. Hedging in this manner therefore requires consideration of the prices of the two binaries in order to short just enough of the upper strike to ensure the P&L does not become negative.

Of course this approach can be mitigated by 'running' the long naked and hedging with a higher strike once the initial trade is in profit. For example, if one were to go long an upbet at 50, then watch the underlying rise to the next higher strike and then sell the higher strike upbet at 50, then it now becomes impossible to lose although if the underlying kept on rising the profit would be zero. In this scenario the trader has 'legged' into the rangebet consisting of the lower and upper strike for zero.....and traders should never sniff at the chance of buying options for zero.

10.4.2 Short Rangebet Hedged with Long Rangebet

Selling the $99.50/$100.50 rangebet could be hedged by buying the $99/$101 rangebet. If this hedge was put on after the initial rangebet was run into a profit, i.e. the underlying has moved away from the strikes, a profit could be locked in the same manner as legging the upbet with a short upbet at 50.

Any strategy trade consisting of a combination of upbets and downbets, i.e. rangebets and eachwaybets, can always be hedged out of by executing opposite trades of the strategy's component parts. An eachway upbet consists of a short downbet and long upbet so if one is long the eachway upbet then by shorting the same strike upbet or going long the downbet starts to close out the eachwaybet. The only problem is that this may well generate risk in certain scenarios as closing one leg of the eachway upbet automatically involves running the other leg naked.

10.5 Summary

As initially proposed in the introduction, hedging is an art form unless one is 100% reversing the open position. Any form of offsetting risk can be considered a hedge although in circumstances a localised hedge (reducing delta, for instance) may generate greater risk away from the current underlying price. The terminology 'hedging' in order to decrease risk should be considered warily since decreasing the localised risk only to create a greater and possibly show-stopping risk elsewhere could be considered foolhardy; hedging to flatten out the current 'greeks' can easily throw up a smokescreen and hide the portfolio risk of a position.

10.6 Exercises

1. A trader sells the $99/$101 rangebet trading at 75. A number comes out and the underlying rallies to $102 where the $102 upbet is trading at 50.

   a) Would buying or selling the upbet hedge the rangebet's winning position or stop out the rangebet's losing position?

183

b) If the trader were to sell the upbet is he/she guaranteeing locking in a profit or a loss?

c) If profit, what is the profit the trader is guaranteeing?

d) What is the potential maximum profit of the position now?

2. A trader sells the $99/$101 rangebet and wants a localised hedge using the $98/$102 conventional strangle.

a) Should the trader buy or sell the strangle?

b) What is the maximum profit possible?

c) What is the maximum loss possible?

3. A trader sells the at-the-money $100 upbet and buys the $100 conventional call with the same expiry. The market rallies to $102. Is this position guaranteed to be profitable?

4. A trader is short the underlying at $100, $10/pt. To hedge he buys the at-the-money $99 upbet for 50 for $10/pt.

a) At the upbet's expiry the underlying is trading at $98. What is the traders P&L?

b) On the upside where is the trader's breakeven after the hedge is bought?

c) What is the maximum downside of the position after the hedge?

10.7 Answers

1. a) Selling the upbet will hedge the position. Remember, selling the rangebet means you want the underlying outside the strikes as in effect you are buying the $99 downbet and buying the $101 upbet.

b) If the trader sells the upbet at 50 a profit is guaranteed.

c) The rangebet can still lose 25 (75-100) should the underlying fall and expire between the strikes. If it did so then the the this loss would be offset by the premium of 50 received from the upbet to guarantee a profit of 25. Also, if the underlying finishes above $102 the upbet loses 50 but the rangebet settles at 0 yet again accruing a guaranteed profit of 25.

d) The maximum profit will be below $99 or between $101 and $102 where a profit of 125 will be made, as the rangebet and upbet both expire worthless.

2. a) Sell the strangle.

  b) The maximum profit would occur between $98 and $99 and between $101 and $102 where the trader receives both the rangebet and strangle premium.

  c) There is no maximum loss as the loss is unlimited on the upside by the naked short call component of the short strangle.

3. a) Yes, the position is guaranteed to be profitable since the upbet is at-the-money and can only lose 50 while the conventional call has to be worth 200 points of intrinsic value, so unless the trader paid more than 150 for the conventional call the position has to be profitable.

4. a) The underlying will make a profit of $200 \times \$10/pt = \$2,000$. The upbet loses $50 \times \$10/pt = \$500$. So the total P&L is a profit of $1,500.

  b) The breakeven is now at $100.50. Prior to buying the upbet the breakeven was $100 but the 50 profit from the upbet means that the underlying can rise to $100.50 before a loss is incurred.

  c) The maximum downside is unlimited as there is now no cover for the naked short underlying position above $100.50.

Section IV:

This section covers one-touch upbets and downbets and no-touch rangebets.

One-touch and no-touch bets are not concerned with the outcome of the event at the expiry of the bet but with the path of the event during the life of the bet. A bet can win and lose at any time leading up to and including the expiry of the bet although the likelihood of the underlying hitting the strike at exactly the same instant as the bet expires is in reality highly unlikely.

In conventional options parlance, as much as upbets can be described as European binary calls, a one-touch upbet can be similarly described as an American binary call. European options cannot be exercised prior to the expiry of the option whereas an American option can be exercised at any time during the life of the option at the long's discretion. But once the one-touch has reached the strike it would be worth 100, and at that point since the bet's value cannot get any higher there is absolutely no point in owning the bet for a moment longer so it would be exercised immediately. Since it is recognised that one-touches all display this feature it is generally written into the contract specification that the bet ends the instant the strike is touched or breached.

In the course of this section the term 'one-touch' and 'no-touch' refer to bets that not only win or lose immediately on touching, but also settle that day as well. One-touches in the course of this book are not deferred options where the bet is settled on the expiry date.

One-touch and no-touch bets create their own administrative problem since the bet needs to be constantly monitored.

Some one-touch and no-touch bets will be constrained by the need for the bet to touch during a particular time zone window since monitoring trading can become prohibitively expensive and unreliable. Furthermore, if the liquidity in the underlying in a particular time zone is unsatisfactory it becomes relatively easy to manipulate the price of the underlying, hence another good reason for one-touch bets being only allowed to win while in particular time zones.

Chapter 11 discusses the evaluation of one-touch upbets and one-touch downbets with analysis of the greeks. Constant comparisons with upbets and downbets are made.

Chapter 12 goes through the same routine for no-touch rangebets. Owing for the need to use a conditional probability evaluation of this bet the different mathematical technique required in evaluating no-touch rangebets is covered at length.

Chapter 13 involves the uses of one-touch upbets and downbets and no-touch rangebets and analyses the different P&L profiles of these bets.

Chapter 13 is on one-touch and no-touch hedging and illustrates ways the trader can use the underlying, conventional options and upbets and downbets to create different structures in order to maximise the trader's profit profile.

11

One-Touch UpBets & DownBets

11.0   Introduction

Examples of 'one-touch' bets are:

1. Will the Sep/Mar Eurodollar spread ever trade 20 ticks or more apart?

2. Will WTI oil trade up to $150 or more by the end of next year?

3. Will WTI oil trade down to $100 by the end of next June?

4. Will the price of the September US 10 year Notes futures rise to trade at or higher than $118?

The event, i.e. oil trading at $150 or higher only needs to happen once, for a split second, and the bet immediately becomes a winner or loser (no 'dead-heats'). For this reason one-touch upbets and downbets are more of a gambler's instrument than the regulars as the one-touch is really not a hedging instrument at all. Indeed, one-touch bets may be perfect for hedge funds!

11.1   One-Touch Upbet Specification

Fig 11.1.1 shows random walks generated for one-touch upbets starting with an underlying price of $100, twenty-five days to expiry and a strike price of $101. The random walks are identical to the random walks generated for upbets in Fig 1.1.1 so that a comparison between winning and losing upbets and one-touch upbets can be made.

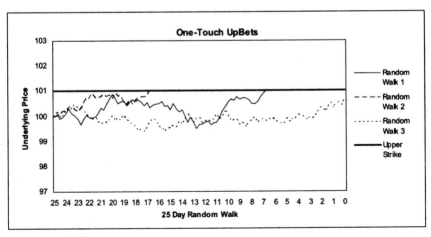

Figure 11.1.1

1. RW1 rises to the $101 level after eighteen days, trades ('touches') $101 and is therefore a winning bet.

2. After eight days RW2 rises to touch $101 and this 'one-touch' upbet is a 'winner'.

3. RW3 is never 'at the races' drifting sideways before making a forlorn effort with three days to expiry but still only reaching $100.50. A loser.

One-Touch Upbets	Lose (0)	Win (100)
Random Walk 1		✓
Random Walk 2		✓
Random Walk 3	✓	

11.2 One-Touch Upbet Pricing

Fig 11.2.1 illustrates the expiry price profile of a one-touch upbet. The difference between this profile and the upbet's of Fig 1.2.1 is there is no 'dead heat' possibility where the underlying finishes exactly on the strike. The definition of a 'dead heat' when applied to a one-touch upbet clearly defines a winning bet.

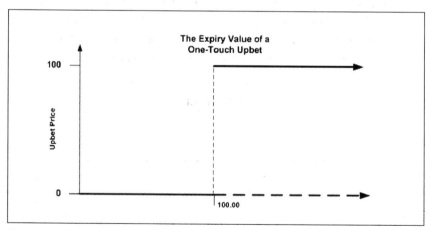

Figure 11.2.1

This provides a direct relationship between the upbet and the one-touch upbet when they both have the same strike and time to expiry (providing implied volatility and time to expiry are not extremely high). When the underlying is exactly on a strike the upbet is worth 50, yet this same condition defines a winning one-touch upbet which is consequently worth 100. The one-touch upbet is therefore worth twice the upbet when the one-touch wins so that arbitrage will generally ensure that if the one-touch upbet is worth double the upbet at the strike then it will be worth double at all other times. For example, if a trader pays 25 for both the same strike and expiry upbet and one-touch upbet, then on the under-lying rising to exactly the strike price the upbet will be worth 50 while the one-touch upbet will be worth 100, i.e. the upbet has returned a 100% profit while the one-touch upbet has returned a 400% profit. The trader would therefore buy the one-touch upbet and sell upbets until they return the same percentage profit. The upbet will get sold down to 20 while the one-touch upbet will be bought up to 40 at which point the upbet will make a profit of 50/20 = 250%, while the one-touch upbet will make a profit of 100/40 = 250%. Obviously the one-touch upbet is worth double the upbet at that point and this relationship must endure.

11.3   One-Touch Upbet Profit & Loss Profiles

The purchaser of the one-touch bet as with any other option can only lose the amount spent on premium. If in the above example Trader A paid 25 for the one-touch upbet at $1 per point then Trader A can lose a maximum of just 25 x $1 = $25. Fig 11.3.1 illustrates the P&L profile for Trader A.

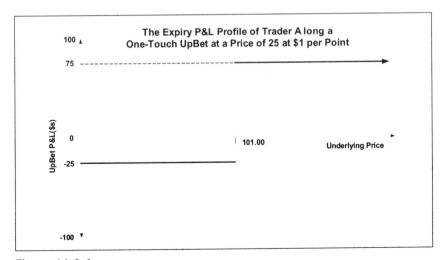

Figure 11.3.1

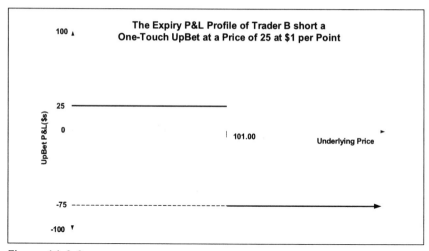

Figure 11.3.2

Trader B has sold this one-touch upbet for 25 at $1/pt so conversely Trader B's P&L profile is, as one would expect, the mirror image of Trader A's reflected through the horizontal axis as in Fig 11.3.2. Trader B pockets the $25 if the underlying never reaches $101, but loses $75 if it does.

11.4 One-Touch Downbet Specification

Fig 11.4.1 presents the random walks generated for one-touch downbets starting with an underlying price of $100, twenty-five days to expiry and a strike price of $99. The random walks are identical to the random walks of Fig 1.4.1.

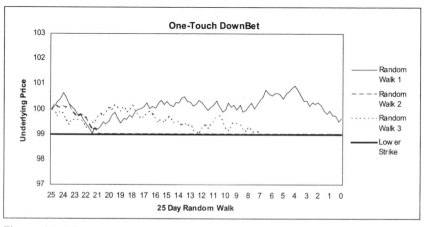

Figure 11.4.1

1. RW1 brushes but does not touch the strike after three days, subsequently rallies and never gets close to touching the strike again. A loser worth zero.

2. RW2 falls to the $99 level after four days. It is a 'winner' and settles at 100.

3. RW3 very slowly drifts down to trade $99 with 7 days to expiry. RW3 is a winner and also settles at 100.

11.5 One-Touch Downbet Pricing

Fig 11.5.1 illustrates the expiry price profile of a one-touch downbet, strike $99.

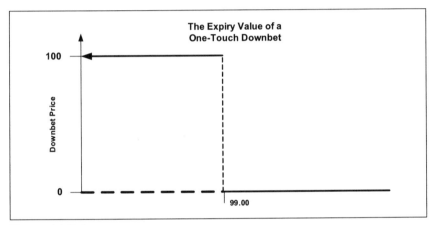

Figure 11.5.1

As with the one-touch upbet there is no 'draw' or 'dead heat' settlement at 50.

11.6 One-Touch Downbet Profit & Loss Profiles

Fig 11.6.1 illustrates the one-touch P&L profile for Trader A who has bought the $99 one-touch downbet for 75. Although A's gone long at 75 (above 50) this one-touch downbet is still out-of-the-money.

Obviously the seller of this bet has a P&L profile exactly as Fig 11.6.1 except reflected through the horizontal axis.

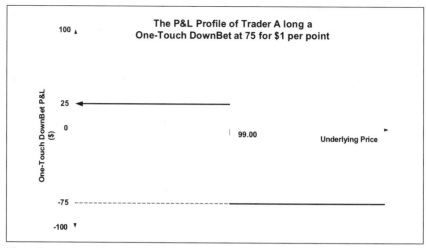

Figure 11.6.1

It should be clear that a long one-touch downbet is not the same as being short the one-touch upbet. In fact they cannot even exist coincidentally. For example, a long position in the $100 one-touch downbet means that the underlying is above $100, otherwise the bet will have settled and ceased to exist. On the other hand the one-touch $100 upbet cannot exist above $100. The bets are mutually exclusive.

11.7   One-Touch Upbet Theta θ & Time

This section covers how one-touch upbets deteriorate in value over time. Most of the theory follows on from Section 2.2 covering time decay and theta but with a couple of interesting differences.

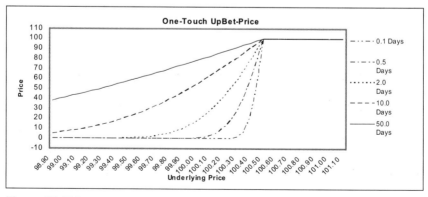

Figure 11.7.1

As Fig 11.2.1 illustrated, the discontinuous price profile of the one-touch upbet is the same as for the upbet but without the possibility of a 'dead-heat' with the subsequent settlement price of 50. Fig 11.7.1 displays how this impacts price over time for the $100.50 one-touch upbet.

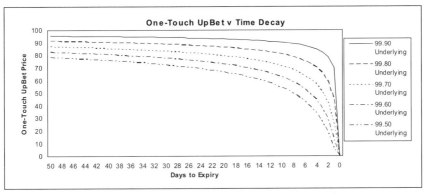

Figure 11.7.2

Fig 11.7.2 plots one-touch upbets with a volatility of 5% and a strike price of $100 against time decreasing from 50 days to zero. The graph offers a direct comparison with Fig 2.2.1, the difference being in scale. On comparing the gradients of Figs.11.7.2 and 2.2.1, it should be apparent that if with 50 days to expiry the one-touch upbet is double the price of the upbet, and that at any time leading up to expiry this relationship persists, then the gradient of the one-touch upbet must be twice that of the upbet if they are both to be worth zero at expiry.

Table 11.7.1 shows values of one-touch upbets and upbets with 1 and 2 days to expiry and a volatility of 5% assuming a strike price of $100.

Upbet Prices		Underlying Price				
		$99.50	$99.60	$99.70	$99.80	$99.90
Reg	1	2.7645	6.2666	12.5210	22.1757	35.0638
	2	8.7523	13.9014	20.7930	29.3647	39.2745
1-T	1	5.5317	12.5403	25.0583	44.3848	70.1894
	2	17.5196	27.8291	41.6295	58.7979	78.6520

Table 11.7.1

Table 11.7.2 provides 1.5 day thetas for the bets in Table 11.7.1. The theta for a one-touch upbet is almost exactly double the equivalent regular upbet theta.

Upbet Thetas		Underlying Price				
		$99.50	$99.60	$99.70	$99.80	$99.90
Reg	1.5	−22.2685	−27.6813	−29.2278	−24.8550	−14.3489
1-T	1.5	−44.5826	−55.4336	−58.5558	−49.8379	−28.8460

Table 11.7.2

How accurate is the 1.5 day theta in evaluation of the time decay between day 2 and day 1? From Table 11.7.1 at $99.70 the one-touch upbet loses:

$$25.0583 - 41.6295 = -16.5712 \text{ points.}$$

The corresponding theta from Table 11.7.2 shows a theta of −58.5558. This indicates a one-day decay of:

$$100 \times - 58.558 / 365 = - 16.0427 \text{ points.}$$

The one-touch theta is out by just over .5 point with 1.5 days to expiry, a percentage discrepancy of:

$$(16.5712 - 16.0427) / 16.5712 = 3.19\%$$

which is probably accurate enough for most risk analysis. The error of 3.19% is due to the increase in error as time to expiry runs out and so one may expect a relatively high discrepancy with only 1.5 days left. The more time to expiry, the more accurate the theta.

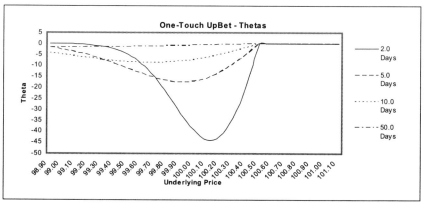

Figure 11.7.3

Fig 11.7.3 illustrates how thetas change with the underlying. The assumed strike price is $100.50 with 5% vol and four separate times to expiry are displayed. Yet again it is apparent how little effect time has on the price of an upbet with 50 days to expiry with the 50-day profile being almost flat around the zero theta level. Another point of note is that theta is always negative or zero.

11.8 One-Touch Downbet Theta θ & Time

Figs 11.8.1 and 11.8.2 provide examples of a one-touch $99.50 downbet showing decay over time plus the corresponding thetas. The same comments made on one-touch upbet prices over time and theta may be applied to the one-touch downbets.

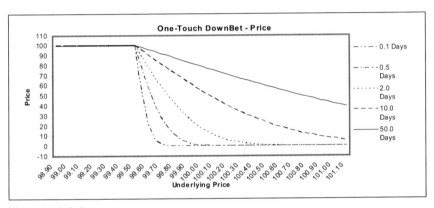

Figure 11.8.1

Unlike the upbet and downbet where theta may be positive or negative dependent on whether the bet is in-the-money or not, the one-touch upbet and one-touch downbet theta are always negative. This will have direct relevance in the section on trading one-touch bets as a strategy to take in time value since the problem encountered in Section 9.3 of the theta switching between a positive and negative value is no longer an issue.

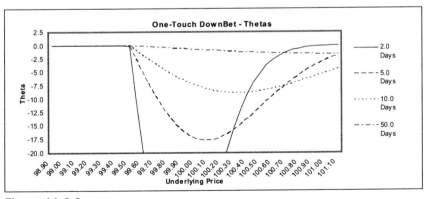

Figure 11.8.2

To summarise, as with out-of-the-money upbets and downbets, one-touch upbets and one-touch downbets generally lose value over time so, although one-touch upbets and one-touch downbets are worth twice upbets and downbets, the one-touches lose time value at twice the rate and hence have a theta double that of the upbet and downbet.

11.9   Extreme Time & One-Touch Theta θ

'Generally lose time' is the accurate expression to use, since once again as time decreases from extreme limits the value of the one-touch upbet increases as Fig 11.9.1 illustrates.

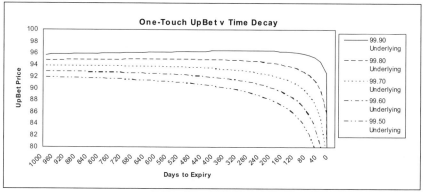

Figure 11.9.1

Nevertheless, the relationship between the one-touch upbet and the upbet remains constant so that with an underlying of $99.90, a strike of $100, volatility of 5% and days to expiry of 1,000, the upbet is worth 47.8679 and the one-touch upbet exactly double at 95.7358.

11.10   One-Touch Upbet Vega

One-touch upbet vega is conceptually the same as upbet vega so this section will just concentrate on outlining the impact of different volatilities on pricing profiles and illustrating the profiles of one-touch vegas.

In general an increase in implied volatility increases the value of five-day one-touch upbets as illustrated in Fig 11.10.1. Since in-the-money one-touches cannot exist, the profile is the same as the upbet profile to the left of the strike, but with the one-touch profiles twice the price for a given time to expiry and implied volatility.

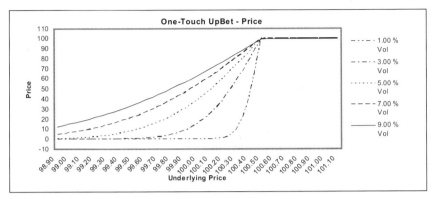

Figure 11.10.1

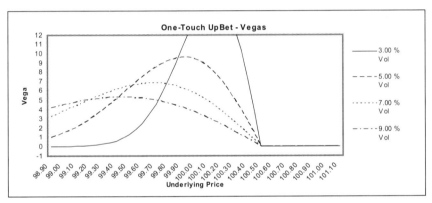

Figure 11.10.2

Upbet Prices		Underlying Price				
		$99.25	$99.50	$99.75	$100.00	$100.25
Reg	1	2.7645	6.2666	12.5210	22.1757	35.0638
	2	8.7523	13.9014	20.7930	29.3647	39.2745
1-T	1	5.5317	12.5403	25.0583	44.3848	70.1894
	2	17.5196	27.8291	41.6295	58.7979	78.6520

Table 11.10.1

Fig 11.10.2 illustrates one-touch upbet vegas which, below the strike, exhibit the same characteristics as the upbet vega except that the one-touch is double the regular vega below the strike and zero above. The fact that the one-touch upbet vega is always positive (or zero) and never switches to negative will possibly be considered to provide the trader with a better instrument for putting on volatility trades than the regular upbet.

Table 11.10.1 illustrates vegas for 5% volatility and a $100.50 strike. Apart from smallish rounding errors it is fairly clear that one-touch upbet vegas are double upbet vegas at this volatility level.

11.11   One-Touch Downbet Vega

Fig 11.11.1 illustrates the impact of implied volatilities ranging from 5% to 45% on the 50-day one-touch downbet, while Fig 11.11.2 provides the corresponding vegas.

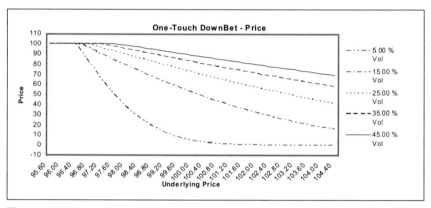

Figure 11.11.1

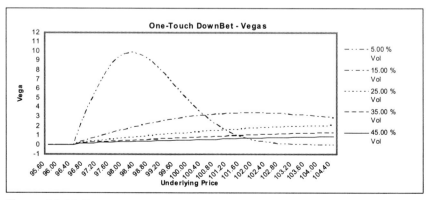

Figure 11.11.2

The range of the underlying is a great deal wider to accommodate the higher volatilities of this example. Of note is the 45% volatility profile which never rises above 1 and is the culmination of increasingly shallow vega profiles as volatility rises from 5% to 45%.

Table 11.11.1 shows 25 and 100-day, 25% volatility vegas for the $96.40 strike downbet showing that for either 25 or 100 days to expiry the one-touch vega is exactly double the regular vega.

Downbet Vega		Underlying Price				
		$96.80	$97.60	$98.40	$99.20	$100.00
Reg	25	0.1531	0.3496	0.5316	0.6915	0.8234
	100	0.1548	0.2552	0.3533	0.4483	0.5389
1-T	25	0.3063	0.6993	1.0632	1.3829	1.6469
	100	0.3096	0.5103	0.7067	0.8965	1.0779

Table 11.11.1

11.12 One-Touch Upbet Delta

Fig 11.12.1 illustrates 5-day one-touch upbet deltas with a strike of $100.50.

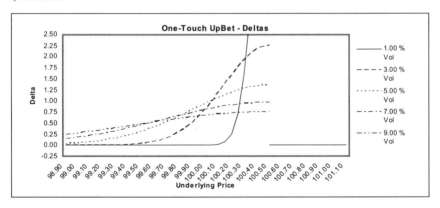

Fig 11.12.1

The delta is a discontinuous variable. When the underlying rises to touch the strike, the delta has value dependant on the implied volatility. On the underlying touching the strike the delta falls precipitously to zero. This has important implications when hedging.

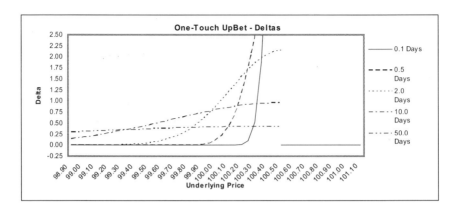

Figure 11.12.2

Fig 11.12.2 illustrates one-touch deltas as time decreases. Yet again the similar effect of time decay and fall in implied volatility are evident.

The one-touch upbet delta is always positive and, as can be seen from Table 11.12.1, is always twice the corresponding regular upbet delta.

Downbet Vega		Underlying Price				
		$99.25	$99.50	$99.75	$100.00	$100.25
Reg	5	0.0020	0.0197	0.1166	0.4133	0.8802
	10	0.1927	0.2366	0.2774	0.3105	0.3320
1-T	5	0.0040	0.0394	0.2333	0.8273	1.7627
	10	0.3868	0.4752	0.5574	0.6243	0.6681

Table 11.12.1

11.13 One-Touch Downbet Deltas

One-touch downbet deltas are always negative and double the corresponding regular downbet delta.

Fig 11.13.1 provides the 25-day $99.50 strike one-touch downbet deltas while Fig 11.13.2 provides the 25% volatility $96.40 one-touch downbet deltas. When comparing the absolute values of the one-touch upbet deltas with the one-touch downbet deltas, the delta values at the strike are very much greater for the shorter term and lower volatility upbets than the downbets. This will provide an interesting hedging problem on the later section on hedging one-touches.

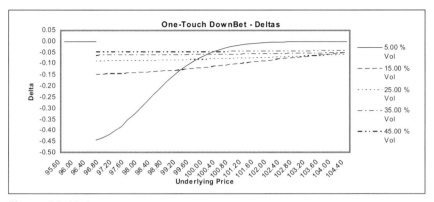

Figure 11.13.1

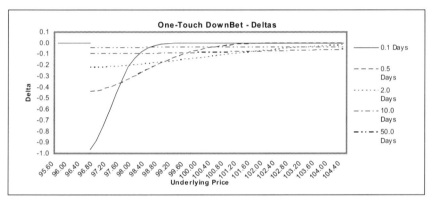

Figure 11.13.2

11.14 One-Touch Upbet Gamma

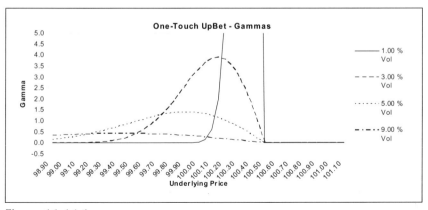

Figure 11.14.1

One-touch upbet gamma measures the slope of the one-touch upbet delta. It tells us how quickly the one-touch delta is changing over a change in the underlying. The one-touch gamma is not discontinuous but falls to zero at the strike.

Figs 11.14.1 and 11.14.2 illustrate $100.50 strike 5% volatility and 5-day one-touch gammas respectively.

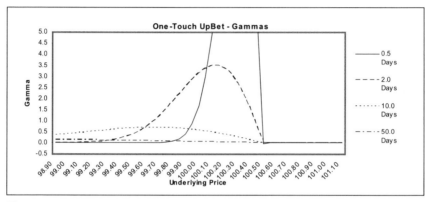

Figure 11.14.2

11.15 One-Touch Downbet Gamma

Since the slope (not the delta itself) of the one-touch downbet delta is always positive the gamma of the one-touch downbet is also always positive. One-touches are always out-of-the-money and out-of-the-money options always have a positive gamma.

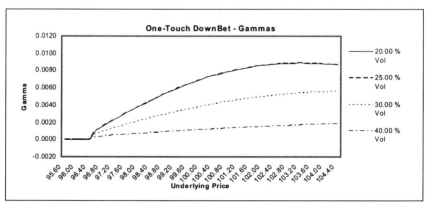

Figure 11.15.1

Figs 11.15.1 and 11.15.2 illustrate one-touch gammas for downbets with 25% volatility and 25 days to go to expiry. With both graphs it is worth reflecting on the left-hand scale and also the range of the underlying.

Clearly by increasing both the time to expiry and volatility the gamma is reduced significantly thereby defining, in terms of the underlying, a much lower profile risk bet.

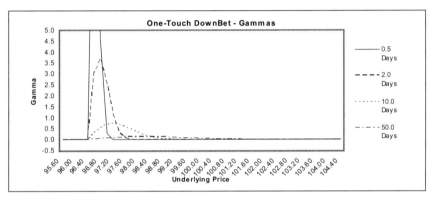

Figure 11.15.2

11.16 Formulae

The formulae for pricing one-touch upbets and one-touch downbets can be simply two times the formulae of Section 1.8 as has already been established, when out-of- or at-the-money the one-touch upbet is always twice the regular upbet. Alternatively the pricing formulae are:

One-Touch Upbet/Binary Call $\quad = \quad \left(\frac{E}{S}\right)^{2r/\sigma^2} N(d_3) + \frac{S}{E} N(d_1)$

One-Touch Upbet/Binary Put $\quad = \quad \left(\frac{E}{S}\right)^{2r/\sigma^2} N(-d_3) + \frac{S}{E} N(-d_1)$

where $\quad = \quad d_1 = \dfrac{\log(\frac{S}{E}) + (r - D + \frac{1}{2}\sigma^2)t}{\sigma\sqrt{t}}$

$$d_3 = \frac{\log(\frac{S}{E}) - (r + \frac{1}{2}\sigma^2)t}{\sigma\sqrt{t}}$$

and
$\quad$ S $\quad = \quad$ price of the underlying

$\quad$ E $\quad = \quad$ strike/exercise price

$\quad$ r $\quad = \quad$ risk free rate of interest

	D	=	continuous dividend yield of underlying
	t	=	time in years to expiry
	σ	=	annualised standard deviation of asset returns.

11.17 Finite Difference & Greeks

Differential calculus is beyond the scope of this book and definitely beyond the mathematical ability of the author so in establishing the value of the greeks for the illustrations in this chapter Finite Difference methodology is used. This involves calculating two prices (or deltas in the case of the gamma) of the one-touch either side of the current price and this process was used in Table 2.2.1 when calculating the theta. The smaller the increment is, the more accurate the approximation is to the actual greek.

Theta

If the increment in time is $\delta t = 0.00001$ of 1 day, then if there are 5 days to expiry the price of the one-touch upbet will be calculated at 4.99999 days and at 5.00001 days.

Then	θ	=	$\dfrac{(P_1 - P_2)}{2\delta t} \times 100$
where	P_1	=	One-Touch Upbet price with 4.99999 days to expiry
and	P_2	=	One-Touch Upbet price with 5.00001 days to expiry.

Example 1:

	S	=	100
	E	=	100.5
	r	=	0
	D	=	0
	Days	=	5
	Vol	=	5%

Therefore	t_1	=	$4.99999/365 = 0.013698603$
and	t_2	=	$5.00001/365 = 0.013698658$
leading to	P_1	=	0.39308069
and	P_2	=	$0.39308163.$

$$\text{Therefore} \quad \theta = \frac{(0.39308069 - 0.39308163) \times 100}{2(0.00001)}$$

$$= -4.717421.$$

Vega

If the increment in volatility is $\delta\sigma = 0.00001$ and if volatility is 5%, the price of the one-touch upbet will be calculated at 5.00001% and at 4.99999%.

$$\text{Then} \quad V = \frac{(P_1 - P_2)}{2\delta\sigma} \times 100$$

where	P_1	=	One-Touch Upbet price with 5.00001% vol
and	P_2	=	One-Touch Upbet price with 4.99999% vol.

Example 1:

	S	=	100
	E	=	100.5
	r	=	0
	D	=	0
	Days	=	5
	Vol	=	5%

Therefore	σ_1	=	5.00001
and	σ_2	=	4.99999
leading to	P_1	=	0.39308211
and	P_2	=	0.39308022.

$$\text{Therefore} \quad V = \frac{(0.39308211 - 0.39308022) \times 100}{2(0.00001)}$$

$$= 9.434841.$$

Delta

If the increment in the underlying is $\delta S = 0.00001$ and if the underlying is 100 the price of the one-touch upbet will be calculated at 99.99999 and at 100.00001.

Then	Δ	=	$\dfrac{(P_1 - P_2)}{2\delta S}$
where	P_1	=	One-Touch Upbet price at 100.00001
and	P_2	=	One-Touch Upbet price at 99.99999.

Example 1:

	S	=	100
	E	=	100.5
	r	=	0
	D	=	0
	Days	=	5
	Vol	=	5%
Therefore	S_1	=	100.00001
and	S_2	=	99.99999
leading to	P_1	=	0.39309064
and	P_2	=	0.39307168.
Therefore	Δ	=	$\dfrac{(0.39309064 - 0.39307168)}{2(0.00001)}$
		=	0.94781.

Gamma

The gamma is the slope of the delta, therefore to calculate the gamma from finite difference methodology one needs to calculate the delta either side of S. If the increment in the underlying is $\delta S = 0.00001$ and if the underlying is 100, the price of the one-touch upbet will be calculated at 99.99999, 100 and at 100.00001.

Then	Δ	=	$\dfrac{(P_1 - P_2)}{2\delta S}$

where	P_1	=	One-Touch Upbet price at 100.00001
and	P_2	=	One-Touch Upbet price at 100.00
and	P_3	=	One-Touch Upbet price at 99.99999.

Example 1:

S	=	100
E	=	100.5
r	=	0
D	=	0
Days	=	5
Vol	=	5%

Therefore	S_1	=	100.00001
and	S_2	=	100.00
and	S_3	=	99.99999
leading to	P_1	=	0.39309064
and	P_2	=	0.39308116
and	P_3	=	0.39307168.

Therefore	Δ_1	=	$\dfrac{(0.39309064 - 0.39308116)}{0.00001}$
		=	0.947816

and	Δ_2	=	$\dfrac{(0.39308116 - 0.39307168)}{0.00001}$
		=	= 0.947803.

Therefore	Γ	=	$\dfrac{(0.947816 - 0.947803)}{0.00001}$
		=	1.377491.

Alternatively one can take the out-of-the-money greek for the equivalent regular upbet and downbet and multiply it by two to get the one-touch version.

The finite difference method of establishing the greeks is essential to the options trader who wants a way of managing their risk by building their own models, whether simple spreadsheet stuff or more sophisticated algorithms, since this method can always be used to check whether the more sophisticated modelling is throwing out roughly the right answers. The author always has parallel calculations based on finite difference methods which are then turned off once experimental short cuts in the more sophisticated models are proven to be accurate.

11.18 Summary

1. One-touch upbets and downbets are twice the price of the same strike and expiry upbet and downbet.

2 One-touch upbets and one-touch downbets with same strike and expiry are mutually exclusive. They cannot both exist at the same time.

3. One-touch bets require an underlying and the ability to constantly monitor that underlying in order to see if the bet has won or not.

4. A conventional American option permits the buyer to control when exercise takes place, the writer being subordinate to the buyer in the exercise mechanism. The one-touch upbet does not confer on the buyer this right. Both buyer and seller of the one-touch upbet are subordinate to the market itself since the market movement of the underlying is what will determine when the one-touch upbet expires.

11.19 Exercises

1. a) The theta of the one-touch upbet is always positive. True or False?

   b) The vega of the one-touch upbet and one-touch downbet is always positive. True or False?

   c) As the one-touch downbet with 30 days to expiry has more time value than the same one-touch with 10 days to expiry, the 30-day bet has a larger absolute theta than the 10-day. True or False?

   d) A one-touch upbet is approaching the strike. The bet would have greater gearing if the implied volatility was low than if high? True or False?

e) The one-touch downbet always has a negative delta. The underlying is hovering just above the strike. A bet with 1 day to expiry provides greater gearing than a 50-day bet. True or False?

2. Oil is $140. The strike is $150. There is half a year to expiry. Interest rates are 5%. What is the value of the one-touch upbet with implied volatility of 15%, 25% and 35%?

3. Calculate the theta, vega, delta and gamma for Question 2.

11.20 Answers

1. a) False. The theta of the one-touch upbet and the one-touch downbet are both always out-of-the-money and are therefore both always negative

b) True. The vega of the one-touch upbet and one-touch downbet are both always positive as they are yet again out-of-the-money so that an increase in volatility makes it more likely the strikes are hit, therefore the bet will be worth more.

c) Indeterminate. Fig 11.8.2 shows thetas over a range of underlying with different times to expiry. As can be seen they intersect; in the example the 2-day theta has a greater absolute value than the 5-day theta as long as the underlying is below 100.30 but a lower absolute value above 100.30. This is in contrast to conventional theta where the shorter expiry always has a greater theta than the longer expiry.

d) True. The key here is that the underlying is approaching the strike. Fig 11.12.1 illustrates that further away from the strike the lower volatility delta is zero therefore any other volatility would provide greater gearing further from the strike.

e) True. The greater absolute delta provides gearing and from Fig 11.13.2 one can see that the lower the time to expiry the greater the absolute value of the delta.

2.

Volatility	15%	25%	35%
Price	57.104055	70.600110	77.166319

3.

Volatility	15%	25%	35%
Theta	-0.124308	-0.078609	-0.056794
Vega	2.059187	0.883789	0.487652
Delta	0.046974	0.029705	0.021462
Gamma	0.001144	0.000193	0.000033

12

No-Touch
Rangebets

12.0   Introduction

In terms of taking a view on volatility the no-touch rangebet is probably the most efficient of all instruments including conventional straddles and strangles. If the trader wants to sell volatility, which in the conventional sense would require selling at-the-money straddles or strangles, the trader would need to buy, not sell, the no-touch rangebet. This is very much a sudden death approach to trading, but at the same time a very lucrative approach to shorting volatility assuming strikes are not touched.

12.1   Specification

The no-touch rangebet provides the opportunity to back a view on whether the underlying will remain in the corridor between two strikes or not. Once more we revert to our random walks to determine winners and losers where in this example the bettor speculates on whether the underlying will remain between $99 and $101 until expiry. Unlike the one-touch upbet and downbet, where touching the strike means the bet has won, in the case of the rangebet when the underlying touches either strike the bet has lost.

1. RW1 lasts for 15 days until it touches the $99 strike and loses with ten days to expiry.

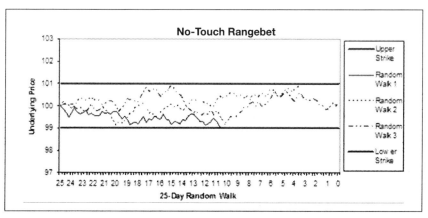

Figure 12.1.1

2. RW2 flirts with the $99 level after five days but then rallies to hit the $101 strike with three days to expiry. It is therefore also a loser.

3. After ten days RW3 nearly gets knocked out when nearly touching the $101 level but then falls to just scrape clear of the $99 level with ten days to expiry. It then has an uneventful ride into expiry and expires with the underlying almost exactly on $100. For the 25 days the underlying has traded within the $99/$101 corridor without touching either levels and is therefore a winning bet.

12.2 No-Touch Rangebet Pricing

Fig 12.2.1 illustrates the expiry profile of the no-touch rangebet. The profile is the same as the regular rangebet's but without the 'dead heat' alternative of the bet settling at 50 exactly on either strike.

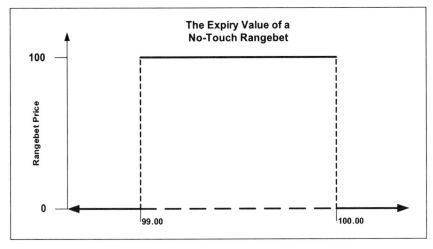

Figure 12.2.1

When one calculates the price of the regular rangebet, the downbet and upbet are added together and subtracted from 100. This methodology does not provide the correct price for the no-touch rangebet. This is because with a regular rangebet if the underlying trades down to the lower strike then the probability of the upper strike being touched or traded through diminishes but does not fall to zero. With the regular rangebet the probability of the underlying trading at the price of the lower strike is independent of whether the underlying trades at the upper strike, and vice versa. With the no-touch rangebet the probability of the underlying trading the lower strike is totally dependent on the underlying not having traded the upper strike, and vice versa.

Furthermore if the price of the one-touch downbet and upbet were aggregated, the result could exceed 100. Once this price is deducted from 100 in order to achieve the probability of the underlying remaining inside the range (as opposed to outside), then the rangebet could take a negative value, clearly impossible. Therefore to correctly establish the fair value of the no-touch rangebet conditional probability techniques are employed; in this particular instance a mathematical solution can be found using an iterative process known as the Fourier theorem.

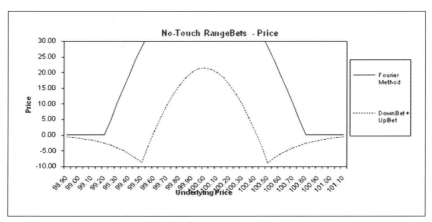

Figure 12.2.2

Fig 12.2.2 compares the two methods of pricing no-touch rangebets using five days to expiry and 5% volatility, and shows the level of inaccuracy provided by using the regular rangebet method of aggregating the downbet and upbet compared with the Fourier method. Clearly if the aggregate solution was used, apart from the nonsense of negative probabilities, the no-touch rangebet price would always be less than the correct value.

12.3   No-Touch Rangebet Theta

Fig 12.3.1 shows the routes to expiry for the regular 99.20/100.80 no-touch rangebet. With 50 days to expiry the profile is flat at almost zero and never exceeds a price of 0.17 of a point. In other words, with 50 days to go to expiry and a volatility of 5%, the odds of the underlying remaining within the $99.20 to $100.80 corridor without ever even touching either strike is nil. As time passes the profiles starts to rise and fill in the rectangle bounded by the rangebet prices of 0 and 100 and the strike prices.

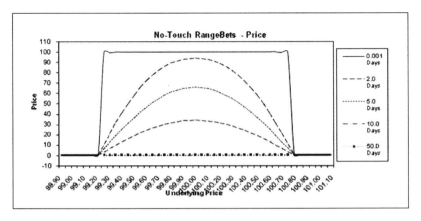

Figure 12.3.1

The mathematical process to evaluate no-touch rangebets involves employing a Fourier series. The Fourier is an iterative process which over- and under-shoots 0 and 100 when very little time to expiry is left. This is known as the Gibbs phenomenon and results in the rather wobbly line in the profile when only 0.001 day are left to expiry. It is not a printer error!

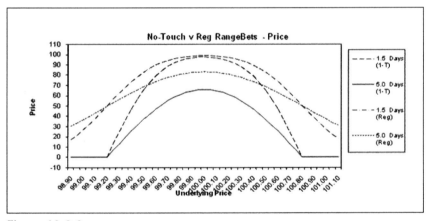

Figure 12.3.2

Fig 12.3.2 illustrates 1.5 and 5-day no-touch and regular rangebet prices assuming strikes of $99.20 and $100.80 and a volatility of 5%. The regular is always worth more than the same expiry no-touch except midway between the strikes, when time to expiry approaches zero where both prices are constrained to 100.

Since there is no direct relationship between the price of a regular rangebet and a no-touch rangebet, there is no direct relationship between their thetas either. Between the strikes the no-touch rangebet theta is graphically of a similar shape to the regular version yet with a higher theta.

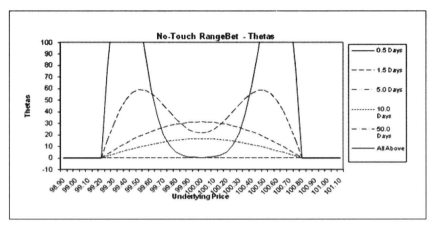

Figure 12.3.3

Fig 12.3.3 and Table 12.3.1 illustrate thetas for the $99.20/$100.80 5% no-touch rangebet and regular rangebet.

Rangebet Thetas		Underlying Price				
		$99.30	$99.65	$100.00	$100.35	$100.70
1-Touch	1.5	29.07	51.27	21.51	51.58	28.65
	5	6.49	24.83	31.22	24.65	6.42
Regular	1.5	14.61	25.66	10.76	25.76	14.25
	5	3.90	12.55	15.64	12.41	3.80

Table 12.3.1

At an underlying of $100 the no-touch rangebet theta falls from 31.22 to 21.51, and from 15.64 to 10.76 for the regular. At $99.65 and $100.35 this pattern is reversed. Clearly theta is influenced not just by time to expiry but very much by the amount of 'elbow room' available for the no-touch rangebet to move in. With half a day to go at $100 the theta is almost zero for no better reason than the price is at its possible highest at 100 points and over the next half day simply cannot accrue more value from an unmoving underlying.

The no-touch rangebet theta is more than the regular theta, which is due to the no-touch rangebet being worth less. In Fig. 12.3.2 with the underlying at $100 there is a price differential of 17.15 points between the 5-day rangebets. At 1.5 days there is a gap of just 1.25 points, so obviously the no-touch rangebet has increased in value 15.90 points more than the regular over the same time period. From Table 12.3.1 at $100 the no-touch rangebet theta is almost double the regular theta for both 1.5 day and 5-day rangebets.

Understanding the profile of no-touch rangebets is of immense importance to those buyers of time decay because the most profitable trades on a daily basis would be long no-touch rangebet positions which are of varying degrees in-the-money. For example in Fig 12.3.3 with 50 days to go it doesn't really matter where the underlying is in relation to the strikes as the buyer will not make a profit over one day. With ten days and five days to go you'd want to be buying the no-touch rangebet if the underlying is at or very near $100. With 1.5 days to go you'd want to buy this rangebet if the underlying was at or near $99.50 or $100.50 and obviously with half a day to go $99.40 and $100.60 offer the greatest thetas.

No-touch rangebets are more of a challenge conceptually but as with financial instruments in general the more complex they are the better chance of making money from them. To that end the conventional premium seller should take a good look at buying no-touch rangebets as they provide many opportunities for taking advantage of time decay.

12.4 No-Touch Rangebet Vega

No-touch rangebets have a similar effect to theta in that as volatility falls it has the same effect on the price profile as time decay. Fig 12.4.1 illustrates profiles for the five-day $99.20/$100.80 no-touch rangebet that obviously has similarities with Fig 12.3.1 which illustrates time decay. The reason for this is that as volatility increases, the odds of the underlying hitting one of the strikes increases which therefore reduces the value of the rangebet.

Fig 12.4.2 illustrates the vega at zero between the strikes at 1% volatility as the no-touch rangebet price has risen to 100. This is similar to the effect of the theta when time decay propels the rangebet price to 100 driving theta down to zero. Similarly when the implied volatility falls and the no-touch rangebet price climbs to 100, then so will vega be driven down to zero as the change in volatility can no longer affect the rangebet price.

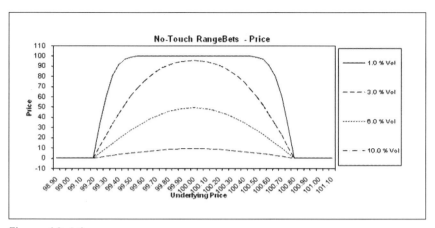

Figure 12.4.1

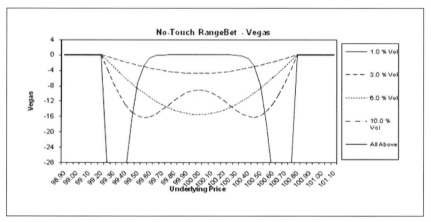

Figure 12.4.2

12.5   No-Touch Rangebet Delta

Figs 12.5.1 and 12.5.2 provide $99.20/$100.80 no-touch rangebet deltas with respectively 5% implied volatility and five days to expiry. No relationship exists between the regular and no-touch rangebet deltas.

Delta-hedging is probably the most commonly used hedging technique with any form of options. The discontinuous nature of the one-touch delta requires that the one-touch trader should fully understand the risks inherent.

The no-touch rangebet has the added complication in that for any pair of strikes the rangebet deltas are both positive and negative within the strikes.

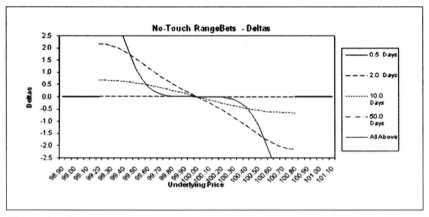

Figure 12.5.1

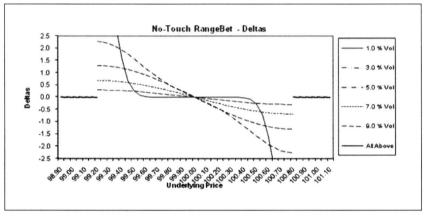

Figure 12.5.2

When trading regulars understanding how deltas work is important; when trading one-touches the additional risks inherent in delta hedging no-touch rangebets requires a thorough understanding of potential delta exposure as the underlying moves outside the strikes.

12.6 No-Touch Rangebet Gamma

As one might expect, as the one-touch upbet and downbet gammas are always positive, so the no-touch rangebet gamma is always negative. If we refer back to the one-touch rangebet deltas in Fig 12.5.1 the deltas move from a positive number at the lower strike, through zero where the underlying is equidistant between the two strikes, to a negative number at the higher strike. The delta always slopes down from left to right, therefore the gamma is always negative, therefore selling rangebets always buys you gamma.

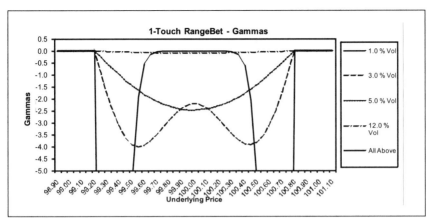

Figure 12.6.1

Fig 12.6.1 illustrates no-touch rangebet gammas for a 25-day bet with strikes at $99.20 and $100.80. At 12% volatility the gamma is almost zero, in turn meaning that the delta is flat (at zero) and that the rangebet is almost worthless. At 12% volatility it is possible for the trader to deduce that the probability of the rangebet winning is almost zero, i.e. that at 12% volatility it is almost certain the underlying will touch one or other of the strikes by expiry simply by looking at the zero gamma. The 25% volatility no-touch rangebet gammas graph has not been included since irrespective of time to expiry the gammas are always zero.

12.7 Formulae

No-Touch Rangebet Value $=$

$$2\pi(\tfrac{S}{E_1})^\alpha \sum_{n=1}^{\infty} n \frac{1 - (-1)^n e^{-\alpha L}}{n^2\pi^2 + \alpha^2 L^2} e^{[-0.5\sigma^2(\frac{\pi n}{L})^2 - \beta]t} \sin(\tfrac{\pi n}{L}\ln\tfrac{S}{E_1})$$

where

S	=	price of the underlying
E_1	=	lower strike/exercise price
E_2	=	upper strike/exercise price
r	=	risk free rate of interest
D	=	continuous dividend yield of underlying
t	=	time in years to expiry

$$\sigma \quad = \quad \text{annualised standard deviation of asset returns}$$

$$\alpha \quad = \quad \tfrac{1}{2} - \left(\frac{r - D}{\sigma^2}\right)$$

$$\beta \quad = \quad r + \tfrac{1}{2}\sigma^2\alpha^2$$

$$L \quad = \quad \frac{\ln E_2}{E_1}$$

$$n \quad = \quad \text{no. of iterations}$$

With most iterative processes the greater the value n above, the more accurate the calculation. The following equation provides the optimal value of n once it has been decided within what level of accuracy the calculation is required to provide.

$$n \quad = \quad \frac{L}{\pi\sigma}\sqrt{-2\beta - \frac{2}{t}\ln\frac{\pi^3\sigma^2 t\varepsilon}{2L^2[1 + e^{|\alpha|L}]}}$$

For instance, if the bet is to be accurate to within 0.005 of a point then enter = 0.00005 into the above equation. The number is 0.005/100 since by convention the binary is the probability multiplied by 100 therefore the error term needs to reflect that in the Fourier calculation. The term $|\alpha|$ is the absolute value of α.

The greeks can be established in exactly the same manner as when using the Finite Difference method in 11.17.

12.8 VBA Code

Here's the VBA code for an Excel spreadsheet for example. The code's not very elegant I don't suppose, but it works.

```
Function NoTouchRangeBet(S As Double, Smin As Double, Smax As Double, Days
As Double, Vol As Double, Rate As Double, Yield As Double, N As Integer) As
Double

Dim sigma As Double, Dim r As Double, Dim d As Double
Dim Agg As Double, Dim Alpha As Double, Dim Beta As Double
Dim L As Double, Dim J As Integer
Dim term1 As Double, Dim term2 As Double, Dim term3 As Double
Dim T As Double
```

```
Dim Value(5000)
Dim NoTouch As Double

T = Days / 365
sigma = Vol / 100
r = Rate / 100
d = Yield / 100
Agg = 0
Alpha = 0.5 - (r - d) / sigma ^ 2
Beta = r + 0.5 * sigma ^ 2 * Alpha ^ 2
L = Log(Smax / Smin)

' Start iterative procedure

For J = 1 To N
    term1 = J * (1 - (-1) ^ J * Exp(-Alpha * L)) / (J ^ 2 * 9.869604401 + Alpha ^ 2 * L ^ 2)
    term2 = Exp((-0.5 * sigma ^ 2 * (3.141592654 * J / L) ^ 2 - Beta) * T)
    term3 = Sin((3.141592654 * J / L) * Log(S / Smin))
    Value(J) = term1 * term2 * term3
    Agg = Agg + Value(J)
Next J

NoTouch = Agg * 2 * 3.141592654 * (S / Smin) ^ Alpha
If NoTouch > 1 Then NoTouch = 1
If NoTouch < 0 Then NoTouch = 0
OneTouchRangeBet = 100 * NoTouch

End Function
```

12.9 Summary

1. There is no relationship between no-touch rangebets and regular rangebets, unlike with one-touch and regular upbets and downbets.

2. Constant monitoring needs to take place to determine whether the bet has won or not.

2. No-touch bets are probably the most efficient way of 'selling volatility'.

3. No-touch bets are a less risky way of 'selling volatility' as the conventional approach of selling straddles and/or strangles creates an unlimited loss scenario.

12.10 Exercises

1. a) The no-touch rangebet delta is greatest midway between the strikes. True or False?

   b) The no-touch rangebet theta is greatest midway between the strikes. Discuss.

   c) The no-touch rangebet vega is greatest midway between the strikes. Discuss.

   d) Gamma is always negative. Why?

2. Those readers familiar with macros and Excel may wish to enter the above VBA code and calculate the value of the no-touch rangebet with:

   S = 99.3, Lower Strike = 99.2, Upper Strike = 100.8, Days to expiry = 5, interest rate = 0, Yield = 0, n = 100.

3. Find the Delta, Gamma, Theta and Vega for the no-touch rangebet in Question 2.

12.11 Answers

1. a) False. The no-touch rangebet delta is always zero midway between the strikes.

   b) The no-touch rangebet theta is greatest midway between the strikes dependant primarily on sufficient time to expiry and furthermore implied volatility. As time to expiry passes, the theta falls due to the no-touch price approaching 100. At this point the theta has a rippling effect whereby the two points of highest theta move away from the strikes mid-point towards the strikes themselves.

   c) The no-touch rangebet vega's always zero or negative and is, in absolute terms, greatest midway between the strikes. This is the opposite effect of theta from Answer 1b) above. With a very low implied volatility and the underlying midway between the strikes the no-touch is unlikely to hit a strike so the bet is worth 100 and the vega therefore falls to zero. As volatility rises there is a greater chance of a strike being hit so the bet is worth less and the vega is negative. As volatility continues to increase the probability of the strikes being hit becomes so high that the bet becomes worthless even midway between the strikes, meaning the vega yet again falls to zero. The absolute value of vega is greatest the lower the volatility and where the underlying approaches either strike.

d) Gamma is always negative or zero because the slope of the delta always slopes down from left to right between the strikes. If volatility is very low then a movement in the underlying from midway between the strikes will have no effect on the no-touch price so the delta is flat at zero with an accompanying zero gamma. Gamma is at its most negative close to the strikes with very low volatility as the delta at both points goes to absolute infinity.

2. No-touch rangebet = 9.6452

3. Delta = 1.278

   Gamma = −0.5268

   Theta = 6.723

   Vega = −3.0698

13

Trading & Hedging 'One-Touch' Bets

13.0   Introduction

The one-touch upbets and downbets only have 50% of the trading opportunities of the regular upbets and downbets. This is because one-touches do not have 'in-the-money' scenarios. This feature is exacerbated for the no-touch rangebet. So, although there are trading opportunities possible for one-touch and no-touch bets they are predominantly punting instruments where the bettor holds on until expiry.

13.1   Punting with One-Touch/No-Touch Bets

One-touch bets can offer the punter a significant advantage over the equivalent regular bets, which is on passing through the strike the bet no longer needs monitoring as it is settled and disappears. One does not need to place overnight orders, for example, to pocket or hedge ones winnings. One-touches need less management, although for some 'hands-on' traders that might not always be attractive.

There is a further real advantage of one-touches in that very often the situation arises where prior to an announcement, e.g. US non-farm payrolls, the options markets are bid up as long-term position holders buy cover. On the figure being announced there is very often a premium sell-off as funds immediately gauge how in or out of line the number is and take advantage of the momentary spike in premium. Very often these announcements/numbers are made at the end of the week in front of the weekend when marketmakers do not want to own premium and lose time decay, so very often the marketmakers lead the sell-off. The situation can then arise that although the punter has called the market right, since he has bought conventional options, his profit is seriously hit by the sharply lower premium from the volatility sell-off. A regular upbet would obviously benefit from such a scenario providing the underlying has passed through the strike and stays above the strike. The one-touch upbet has no concerns as since the strike is hit, the bet settles at 100 and no amount of 'vol bashing' will change that.

The no-touch rangebet is a pure punt on volatility. It may be that prior to an announcement the bettor feels that the market is just very jittery and is going to move irrespective of how erratic the number is. Selling the no-touch then would be a perfect trade should the bettor actually have no view on the direction of the underlying. Alternatively, buying no-touch rangebets in front of long weekends or other times of the year when there is historically little interest in the market, e.g. Thanksgiving, would also be a sound strategy.

13.2 One-Touch v Regular Arbitrage

Conceptually this is a fairly simple trade in that the out-of-the-money regular should always be half the price of the corresponding one-touch bet. If this relationship does not exist then one can lock in a profit (with one significant proviso) by trading one against the other in the ratio of two regular bets to one one-touch bet. But there is a very wrong way and a very right way to put on this trade!

Example 13.2.1

The $117 strike 30-day regular upbet on the 10 year Note is trading at 36.2 while the one-touch is trading at 76, which is too expensive as it should be trading at 36.2 × 2 = 72.4. These would equate to implied volatilities of 6.98% and 8.15%. By selling the one-touch upbet at 76, $10 per point and buying the regular upbet at 36.2 for $20 per point one can lock in a profit. Fig 13.2.1 shows the P&L of this position as time decays and assumes that implied volatility remains constant at 6.98% and 8.15%.

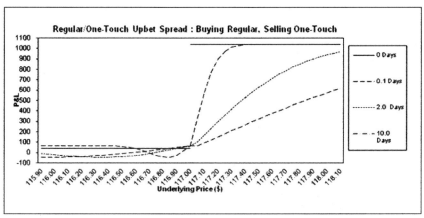

Figure 13.2.1

This is a real 'fill-yer-boots' trade. If the underlying remains below the strike then a guaranteed profit of $36 is made. Not much you might say?

Then stick it on $1,000 per point as this is risk-free money. Although if the underlying stays below the strike, the different time decay owing to the different implied volatilities can generate a losing position; if the trader stays with the position the losses are recouped and a profit guaranteed.

On the other hand, if the underlying starts flying then the short one-touch hits 100 when the long regular bet is worth 50. The trader now owns these regular upbets at an average price of 50–$36/$20 = 48.2, the 50 being the at-the-money price of the upbet, the $36 being the accrued profit at that instant, and the $20 being the stake per point of the regular upbet.

The trader now has three choices:

1. Run the upbet naked and maybe achieve the P&Ls to the right of the strike in Fig 13.2.1.

2. Sell the upbet at 50 and take the $36 profit, or

3. Sell futures at $117 in a delta neutral manner and hope the market plunges.

Whichever way, the trader is in the 'driving seat'. And if the trader had a bit of luck the underlying would have 'gapped up' through the strike leaving him with a further choice, to sell the $117.50 upbet.

If it were possible to enter into this trade prior to the issue of price sensitive data then it is almost akin to picking up free call options. If one can put this trade on for zero credit immediately prior to an announcement and short time to expiry then do it.

What this example suggests is that the one-touch should trade at a lower implied volatility than the regular upbet.

Now compare this scenario to the alternative of buying the one-touch and selling the regular.

Example 13.2.2

The $117 strike 30-day regular upbet on the 10 year Note is trading at 36.2 while the one-touch is trading at 66, which is too cheap as it should be trading at 72.4. These would equate to implied volatilities of 6.98% and 5.54%. Buy the one-touch upbet at 66 for $10 per point and sell the regular upbet at 36.2 for $20 per point. Fig 13.2.2 shows the price profiles

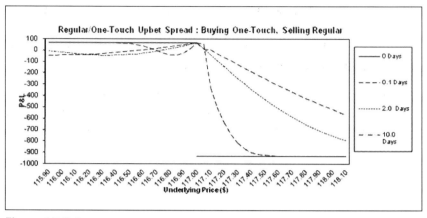

Figure 13.2.2

For the pleasure of making $64 the trader is exposed to a possible loss of $936 which does not provide an attractive risk/return ratio and is not an intelligent trade, and would be even more ludicrous if put on just prior to expiry.

By buying both no-touch rangebets and the same strike regular rangebet, one can achieve similar potentially profitable positions.

13.3   One-Touch v Conventional Options

Fig 13.3.1 illustrates a spread P&L scenario consisting of $100 strike, 10-day, 5% volatility conventional calls and one-touch upbets. The premium to the left of the underlying at $100 shows that the one-touch is more expensive than the conventional call. This is because at the strike the one-touch reflects a win of 100 while the conventional can not even boast of any intrinsic value. The conventional call has to see the underlying a great deal higher before it too is worth 100. At the underlying of $100, the one-touch is worth 100, while the conventional is only worth 33.02. If a trader wanted to buy the conventional and sell the one-touch and break even at $100 then the trader needs to buy the call for approximately 3x the value per point than he sells the one-touch for.

The trader sells the one-touch for $10 per point and buys the call for $30 per point. The worst case scenario is at $99.50 where the spread has lost $128.09 and it takes until an underlying of $100.54 before the spread makes $1000 profit. At the underlying of $100 the spread has lost $9.50.

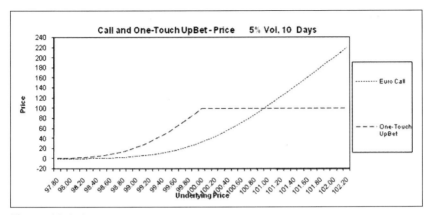

Figure 13.3.1

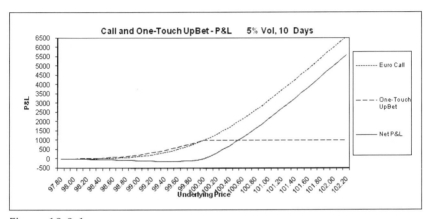

Figure 13.3.1

This just one example of combining one-touches and conventionals to create positions with very limited downside but extremely geared upside. It is not a particularly aggressive trade but for a trader with a huge conviction unmatched by their limited funds it is an expedient way to get long.

13.4   One-Touch v Underlying

Covered warrants involve buying the underlying and selling out-of-the-money conventional calls against them. The idea is that if the underlying market falls the call premium provides a bit of downside protection, although the profits on the upside flatten out above the strike. This section covers the possibility of selling one-touch upbets against a long position in the underlying. The point of this structuring of a position is to show

how one can continuously add on other instruments, regardless of whether the new instruments are regular or one-touch upbets, conventional calls or puts, plus futures.

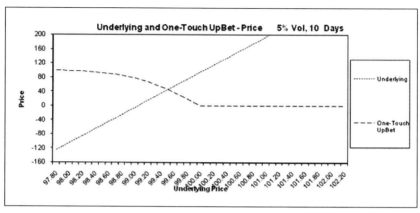

Figure 13.4.1

The non-farm payrolls are about to come out and the punter believes that the premium is expensive. The punter also fancies the market to break up through the $100 level and possibly a lot higher, as he believes there are too many 'shorts' in the market who will need to cover. The punter therefore feels that selling the $100 one-touch upbet at 45.80 and buying futures in a delta neutral manner will take advantage of the rich premium and will be profitable if his hunch is right about a strong rally in the market. The underlying is at present trading around the $99.50 level and the delta of the one-touch upbet is 0.8045. Fig 13.4.1 shows the profile of the short upbet being 100 less the price, while the underlying is depicted by the 45° degree straight line.

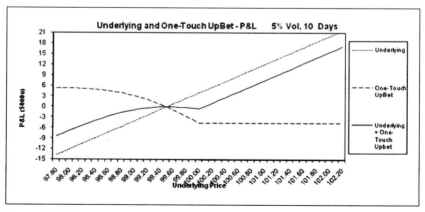

Figure 13.4.2

238

Fig 13.4.2 shows the P&L profiles of the one-touch upbet traded at $100/pt and the underlying traded at $80.45 per point with the aggregate position depicted by the solid line.

Above the strike the aggregate P&L behaves exactly as a long future of $80.45/pt. Around the level of $99.50 the trader loses a small amount, but as the underlying falls and the one-touch premium falls to zero thereby offering no further cover, the position reverts to the profile of a future again.

To cover this liability the trader decides it would be prudent to get some downside cover and buys the $99 conventional put for 13.66 at $100/pt. The price profiles for the three instruments are illustrated in Fig 13.4.3 with the individual and aggregate P&Ls shown in Fig 13.4.4.

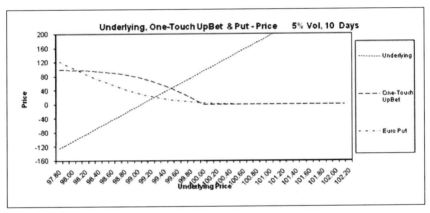

Figure 13.4.3

The solid line in Fig 13.4.4 shows the healthy situation of an increasingly positive P&L as the profile hits the extremes on each side of the graph, yet to pay for this position the maximum downside is just −$1,480 at the strike.

It should be remembered that this position was a strategy explicitly for the announcement of the non-farm payroll; it wasn't a position to run for the 10 days to expiry. As a matter of discipline one should enter into trades/strategies with a preconceived plan; contingencies should already be in place for worst case scenarios, or for that matter best case scenarios. A standard joke across futures markets is the use of the GTC trade which should stand for Good 'til Cancelled. Too often undisciplined traders working a stop loss order would pull their stop as it got close to trading, thus leaving them without a strategy and such ill-disciplined trading can and will end up in disaster. As you can imagine, such traders when issuing GTC orders were invariably asked by the broker (with tongue in cheek) whether the 'C' stood for Cancelled or Close! But it is sometimes worthwhile to take a look at a position to expiry as if by a fluke every scenario was profitable then the decision making process is redundant.

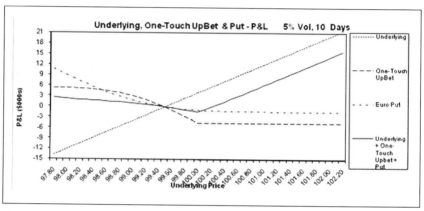

Figure 13.4.4

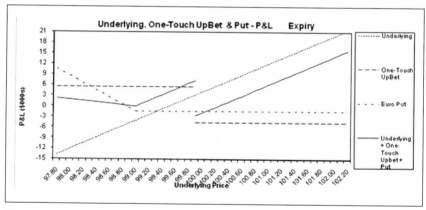

Figure 13.4.5

Fig 13.4.5 shows the expiry P&L profile of the above structured trade. The solid aggregate line is pretty healthy in fact. Below the strike the position always makes a profit, although at the strike the worst case scenario is a loss of $2,730. But remember this loss is if the underlying is exactly $100 at expiry; by $100.24 the position is back in profit. A 24 tick losing window over a 440 tick range might be considered such a solid strategy that it is worth keeping on without regard to the figure.

13.5 Summary

1. One-touch upbets and downbets are essentially bets for the directional speculator.

2. No-touch rangebets are a tool for speculating on volatility.

3. One-touch upbets and downbets are not instruments for trading and hedging with, as the strike can render the hedge a liability.

4. One-touch upbets and downbets can provide the sophisticated trader with the ability to build bespoke solutions to capitalise on market views and convictions.

5. Spreadbetting companies and exchanges that offer one-touch and no-touch products are likely to do so under strict rules as to which time zones and when the strike can be triggered. This is imperative for orderly trading and to ensure that market manipulation is kept to a minimum. (Speaking as a 'local' I never found too much wrong with disorderly markets and market manipulation, food and drink to all well-meaning and upright citizens of trading floors!)

13.6 Exercises

1. Which of these positions are long gamma?

   a) long one-touch upbet

   b) short one-touch downbet

   c) short no-touch rangebet

2. A trader sells the no-touch rangebet in front of a long weekend in which nothing happens and the underlying reopens unchanged. Does implied volatility need to rise or fall to offset the trade'rs theta loss?

3. The theta of a one-touch bet is always positive. True or False?

4. The theta of a no-touch rangebet is always positive. True or False?

13.7 Answers

1. One-touch bets are always long gamma as they are always out-of-the-money. Therefore:

a) is long gamma

b) is short gamma

c) Any rangebet is short gamma between the strikes therefore a one-touch is a short gamma bet. So being short a short gamma bet such as the no-touch rangebet is a long gamma position.

2. If volatility remains unchanged then the no-touch rangebet will be worth more at the start of the new week. To compensate volatility needs to rise to make the no-touch rangebet lose value.

3. False. It is always negative.

4. True. Except when the no-touch has reached the value of 100 when the theta is zero.

Bibliography

Books and papers that were used for background research and formulating ideas from include the following in no particular order:

'Derivatives' by Paul Wilmott: John Wiley and Sons

'Exotic Options' by Peter G. Zhang: World Scientific Publishing

'Options, Futures & Other Derivatives' by John C. Hull: Prentice Hall

'Options Markets' by Cox & Rubenstein: Prentice Hall

'Dynamic Hedging' by Nassim Taleb: John Wiley

'An Analysis of Onion Options and Double-no-Touch Digitals' by S. Ebenfeld, M.Mayr & J.Topper of d-fine GmbH

'One-Touch Double Barrier Binary Option Values' by C.H.Hui: Applied Financial Economics (1996)

Index

25:10:0 spreadbet 122
    deltas 123
    gammas 123
    pricing of 122
    theta 124
    vega124
100:40:0 132, 151

A

arbitrage 234
at-the-money 29, 34

B

bets v conventionals 173
binary options 3
    as a conventional call spread
    168
    as call spreads 168
Black-Scholes 45, 49, 159

C

call spreads 168-171
    conventionals 168, 173-174,
    177, 182
calls 21
carried out 181
central banks 153
chartists 49
Christmas Tree 177
clearing and settlement 5
combo 114
conventional call spreads , see
'call spreads'
conventional options v one-touch
236

covered warrants 237
cylinder 114

D

dead heat 16, 97, 113, 115, 132,
192, 218
delta 65, 79, 147, 151, 171, 182
25:10:0 123
    and gamma 79, 81
    and the gradient of the price
    profile 65
    bets v conventionals 71
    definition 66
    downbet 69
    eachway rangebet 135
    eachwaybet 120
    exercises 7
    finite difference 210
    formulae 72
    gradient formula 66
    hedging 223
    no-touch rangebets 223
    one-touch upbet 204
    one-touch upbet 203
    upbets 67
dexterity 6
differential calculus 208
directional trading 147
discontinuous distribution 15
downbet 13,25
    buying 25
    delta 69
    exercises 25
    formulae 24
    gamma 83, 105

over time 35
pricing 19
profit and loss profile 20
selling 25
specification 18
theta 36
vega 55, 101
versus
    puts 23-24
        formulae 24
        the underlying 172
volatility 54
draw 16

greeks 116
price specification 111
pricing 112
profit and loss profiles 113
sensitivity analysis 116
theta 116, 124
vega 118, 124
Euribor 153
eurodollar 153
exercises 25, 40, 59, 73, 183, 212, 228
expiry 13, 25, 153-155
extreme time 200

E

eachway rangebet 131, 148
    100:40:0 132, 151
    delta 137
    examples 132
    exercises 139
    gamma 138
    greeks 134
    price specification 131
    pricing 132
    profit and loss profiles 133
    sensitivity analysis 134
    theta 134
    vega 136
eachway upbet/downbet 115
eachwaybet 111
    25:10:0 spreadbet 122-125
    and conventional combos 114
    delta 120, 123
    exercises 125
    gamma 121, 123

F

finite difference 210, 226
    delta 210
    exercises 212
    gamma 210
    theta 208
    vega 209
fixed odds bet 3
foreign exchange trading 29
formulae 24, 31, 39, 58, 72, 207, 225
Fourier method/theorem 219-220, 226
fundamentalists 49

G

gamma 79
    25:10:0 123
    and the gradient of delta 79
    bets v conventionals 84
    downbet 83
    eachway rangebet 138

eachwaybet 121
exercises 86
finite difference 210
formulae 80, 85
no-touch rangebet 224
one-touch downbet 206
one-touch upbet 205
upbet 81
Gibbs phenomenon 220
gradients 52
guts 95

H

hedge funds 167
hedging 167
bets with bets 182
delta hedging 223
exercises 183
rangebets with strangles 178
with conventional calls 174
with puts 178
with the underlying 171
historic volatility, see 'volatility'

I

in-the-money 15
in-running 29
implied volatility, see 'volatility'

L

ladder 177
leverage 5
lognormal distribution 47
long upbet hedged with short

upbet 182
losing bet 15

M

marketmakers 39, 54, 79, 81, 125, 162, 181-182
minimax 114

N

no-touch rangebets 217
delta 223
exercises 228
expiry value 218
formulae 225
gamma 224
pricing 218
punting with 233
specification 217
theta 219
vega 222
normal distribution 29, 45, 47

O

OTC, see 'over-the-counter'
one-touch bets 191, 196
downbet
deltas 204
gamma 206
pricing 195
profit and loss profiles 195
specification 194
theta and time 199
vega 202

exercises 241
formulae 207
punting with 233
theta and extreme time 200
upbet
    delta 203
    gamma 204
    pricing 192
    profit and loss profiles 193
    specification 191
    theta and time 196
    vega 200
versus
    conventional options 236
    regular arbitrage 234
    underlying 237
out-of-the-money 15
over-the-counter (OTC) 4

P

price decay
    and theta 30
probability 25
product sets 6
puts 23, 17

R

random walk theory 49
random walks 14, 93, 111, 131, 191, 194, 217
rangebets 93, 148, 173, 217, 221
    delta 103
    eachway 131
    examples of 94-95

exercises 107
expiry profile 94-95
gamma 105
greeks 98
hedging with strangles
long 183
no-touch, see 'no-touch rangebets'
price specification 93
pricing 94
profit and loss profiles 95
sensitivity analysis 98
short 183
theta 98, 221
versus
    conventional strangles 97
    the underlying 173
vega 101
regulation 5
risk management 4

S

scalpers 49
settlement price 16
short rangebet hedged with long rangebet 183
standard deviation 45
strangles 97
    hedging with rangebets 178
strikes 13, 25, 148, 177, 180, 217

T

teenies 153
theta 29, 39, 168
    25:10:0 124

and price decay 30
bets v conventionals 38
definition of 31
downbet 36
eachway rangebet 134
eachwaybet 116
exercises 40
finite difference 208
formulae 39
marketmakers 39
no-touch rangebet 219
of an option 31
one touch and extreme time 200
selling 162
upbet 32, 197-199
tie 16
time decay 29, 222
trading 147
    bets v bets 158
    directional 147
    exercises 162
    volatility 155

U

underlying, the 171-173
upbet 13, 25
    and extreme time 37
    buying 25
    delta 67
    exercises 25
    formulae 24
    gamma 81, 105
    long 182
    pricing 15
    profit and loss profiles 16

selling 25
short 182
specification 14
theta 32
vega 53, 101
versus
    calls 21-23
        formulae 24
    the underlying 171
    the underlying as a function of volatility 50
    the underlying over time 29

V

VBA code 226
vega 45
    25:10:0 124
    and the impact of volatility 51
    and extreme implied volatility 56
    bets v conventionals 57
    downbet 55, 202
    eachway rangebet 136
    eachwaybet 118
    exercises 59
    finite difference 209
    formulae 58
    marketmakers 54
    no-touch rangebet 222
    upbet 53, 200
volatility 45, 51, 155, 217
    and downbets 54
    historic 45, 48-49, 155
    implied 45, 49, 52, 59, 155

external factors 158
extreme 56
selling of 217
skew/smile 158, 161
trading of 155

W

winning bet 15